Journey to Love

by

Janeen Michael-Lanier

Dedication

I dedicate this book, with my sincerest gratitude, to Christ. For it is only because of His loving provision of the tempestuous conditions I needed that I am now found in His wonderful embrace of safety and rest.

I am eternally grateful, God, for my *Journey to Love*, as I now sail each day upon the winds of Your Spirit of Peace.

Acknowledgments

I wish to express my deepest appreciation to my husband, Jeffery Lanier, for his constant support and encouragement and to my wonderful children, Marcus, Janeen, and Roise.

To my father John Moss, Sr., for the wings to fly and to my mother, Joyce Moss, for the inspiring courage to use them.

To my brother John Moss, Jr., and my sister Joyce Richardson, who made growing up a rich pool of cherished memories.

To my pastor and his wife, Dr. Eric and Mrs. Melany Suddith, for the spacious grace to grow under their ministry of the Word they so dearly love.

To my editor, Scott Philip Stewart, Ph.D., for his labor in love, as unto Christ, that brought more clarity to my words.

Table of Contents

Where Was My Love?

I DIDN'T HAVE TO BEG, barter, or steal for love. When I accepted Jesus Christ as my personal Lord and Savior, the Love that I so desperately longed for was inside of me. All I had to do was "accept" and "receive" the awesome gift of love…though I believed more was required. I simply couldn't believe it was that simple. I also doubted God's words to me about this, just as the enslaved children of Israel doubted when Moses told them they would soon be free:

> "…but they did not listen to him because of their discouragement and cruel bondage."
>
> *(Exodus 6:9b NIV)*

For years I lived with the disconnection between the truth of God's Word, which proclaimed His Love for me, and my ability to dwell daily in the confident security that truth inspires. This breach wounded my heart deeply. I craved the passionate embrace of God, yet I felt uncovered and exposed to every cruel dart of guilt and unworthiness that the enemy hurled at me.

For years I resorted to masquerading to cover up the shame I felt in my heart because I felt "invisible" to God. No matter how hard I tried to be good enough to merit His attentiveness, I constantly felt "invisible."

The distress in my heart was so great, and securing God's love seemed so elusive, that I made attempts to cure myself. Unfortunately, I wound up causing myself greater injury as I sought out alternatives that I could intellectually grasp and measure up to. Each substitute for God's love that I gathered failed me miserably. So much precious time and energy was wasted in vain pursuits.

An incredible journey happened as I finally took a step toward God and took hold of His outstretched hands....

Journey to Love!

Nothing to Prove

To ALL OUTWARD APPEARANCES, I looked like a God-fearing girl who had caught the world by the tail. But the truth was that deep inside that girl lay a cruel darkness—my belief that I had to prove that I was worthy of God's love. The *cruelty* was that I believed that through my own efforts and on account of my pain I could become eligible to receive His love. The *darkness* was my belief that God didn't love me at all. I was convinced that I just didn't measure up, and I was determined to beat that challenge head on!

I spent myself trying to *earn* God's (unconditional) love, which He had already freely provided! I was broken, bankrupt, and bowed over from my efforts, all the while desperately trying to hide my heart's fatigue. Some events in my life have caught me by surprise and violated me in ways beyond my ability to stave off. Others I saw coming from afar and allowed them to breach my quarters. As I reviewed my personal journal writings from that time in my life my eyes were opened to this.

The essence of those journal entries evolved into the book you are reading now. Though most entries were recorded neatly in journaling books, quite a few were on scraps of paper stashed in coat pockets, old purses, hat boxes, and in the margins of dozens of books in my library.

Trying to organize all those entries was therapy—a thinly-veiled way for me to deal with my pain. Early on, I was not conscious of what I was doing...personally shedding and publicly sharing my *Journey To Love*. I made myself believe that my desperate passion to gather these bits and pieces of the tales of my life was only for the sake of "order." All the while, though, God was orchestrating all this good, honest, hard work to heal my confusion and despairing brokenness.

As I reviewed ("organized") those raw feelings I had chronicled, I was taking the first firm steps along this new pathway of discovery that would ultimately lead to the "main road" of my life: Intimately knowing God's love for me. I learned that God wanted to give me more of Himself through the deep, indwelling love relationship I desired. He led me to know and understand that *I really am God's beloved daughter*.

What I had always needed and longed for was to know God's love intimately and live out each day in its security. That was the "it" that I had been craving and spending myself to find...yet I had been seeking less and settled for *much* less. It was as if I had an open invitation to a free sumptuous banquet but out of fear, ignorance, or pride I settled for begging on the street for milk money.

God wanted me to cast all my needs—including this need to feel His passionate, eternal embrace–before Him and upon Him. Eventually I discovered that God desired the same deep intimate relationship with me as I desired with Him. And therein lay a cruel dilemma: I would build an impenetrable wall between myself and what I needed and longed for and never let myself be vulnerable enough to let the wall down and receive what I needed and longed for. The very emotional wall I was using to protect myself from what I feared was lurking outside was also suffocating my heart and its voice on the inside. My soul could not break out.

"Giving it **ALL** to God" just seemed too good to be true. I believed that "if anything sounds too good to be true, it usually is." I was very suspicious and, at best, skeptical of God's offer to take away my fear and all of the other things that caused me to put up emotional walls. It just seemed so unreasonable to trust God with *all* that I needed. I had become too conditioned to not asking for what I needed, denying that I needed it, or trying to survive on my own no-nonsense sweat and tears (the old "boot strap" self-sufficiency). Besides, I was so used to disappointment that I was afraid to hope for true love that would satisfy me in the depths of my soul.

I eventually learned the purpose of God's asking me to "give it all to Him," free fall into his arms, abandon myself to trust Him for my needs, and entrust my heart's desires to Him. It was not to frighten me, but rather to create the capacity in me to taste and see that His overtures and commitment to be intimately near me and unconditionally love me were genuine and true.

As I compiled, arranged, and re-read my journal entries I realized that I simply could not mentally and emotionally rearrange the balance of my all-encompassing burden—my darkness, my belief that God did not love me.

I took a lot of bumps and bruises until I admitted my inability (or unwillingness) to ask for the help I needed to navigate safely through my darkness. Deep down I believed (wrongly) that I had no right to ask for the help I needed because I was not worthy to be helped at all!

Time and exposure brought greater challenges, more pain, and an insatiable craving for more than the "milk provision" I had been receiving could ever satisfy. What I craved was to accept that invitation to dine at the feast at the banquet table. Compiling these bits of raw emotion scattered here and there brought me face-to-face with my emotional malnourishment.

So, why the darkness? Lies. And the truth was buried deep under many layers of masks. In hindsight I can see how the masks obstructed my clear view of the Light of Love.

By *mask* I mean a pre-programmed behavior (either conscious or subconscious) intended to overcome mental and/or emotional vulnerability. Think of a mask as a "saving face" and this pre-programmed behavior as "masquerading." I credit my maternal grandmother for my use of the mask analogy because when I would relate to her in this way she would say, "Neen, you're putting me on."

Some masks got stuck on me. Some well-meaning people who saw my conflict and were suffering from their own handed me masks they thought would numb my pain. I chose to wear other masks because I thought they would help me.

Although in my everyday life I pretended to be vulnerable, connected, and transparent, I wasn't. I was guarded, disconnected, and hazily out of touch. When I consciously put on a mask I was attempting to avoid (or mask) mental and emotional vulnerability. But wearing a mask shielded me from what I needed—to feel God's love directly from Him and through others. Masking also facilitated self-abuse and abuse from others. Masking could not protect my heart from what I believed would hurt me. And it was emotionally exhausting and intellectually taxing. *Why?* Because unconditional love isn't logical, and donning a mask painfully boxed me in to pursuing only that which I could logically grasp.

> "*For my thoughts are not your thoughts, neither are your ways my ways,' declares the LORD.*"
>
> (*Isaiah 55:8-9 NIV*)

I will never be able to fully process the dimensions of God's love—neither the soft or the tough sides. The enemy's trick was to mislead me to believe that I was eligibile to dwell daily in the security of God's Love only if I was able to logically grasp each dimension of His Love. This trick worked so well because I knew God as the Great Almighty Judge but not as my Loving Shepherd. This one-sided view caused me to approach God as the "Letter" and not the "Spirit" of the law.

Miraculously, my heart's spirit had been crying out all along between each line of pain and glory in my journal! Journaling was like a prison break that allowed my heart to freely scale the wall. My initial response to seeing this emotionalism was frustration and fear largely because it had sneaked up on me. It was chilling to see my bleating, malnourished state expressed so clearly and frustrating to admit that I lacked the intellectual resources to solve or stop the clamoring of my desperation and pain.

I thought the benefit of journaling was the cathartic (cleansing) exercise of freeing me to share my truest thoughts. Although there was an immediate benefit of "unloading" and "venting," the true benefit came from the fact that the journal entries captured my truest thoughts. With the exception of dreams I would record, each entry was a blinding beam of light. During those moments of writing when all of the circus noise that filled my life was gone, I would emote honestly.

As I advanced in my journal compiling exercise I became more conscious of my conflict. I tried (silently, quickly, and neatly) to align my anguished heart with the array of masks I had been wearing. It produced all-out war! For years, these masks had dwelt in opposition to one another and produced a steady hum of noise that exhausted my subconscious.

Over the years I had learned to cope with and accept the exhaustion. I could rationalize its symptoms: I had three toddlers, so constant fatigue made sense; I loved to organize and serve in my local church plant, so workaholism made sense; my low self-worth, manifested as humility and self-sacrifice, made sense as I chose to silently suffer in my unhealthy marriage for the sake of the fragile, impressionable little ones in my midst.

What was I to do and how was I to bring about a peaceful resolution? For a long period of time I tried to ignore the conflict that raged inside of me or just pretend that I could mediate this volatile conflict. But I couldn't!

And so began my *Journey To Love*. I devoted an exorbitant amount of energy in coping, and all the while the warring masks tried to conceal my passion to discover God's Love. But once I started along the first pathway I could not turn back. How ridiculous and unfair of me to allow pride and fear to consume so much mental and emotional energy to aggressively deny my pursuit! I resented my own desperation and the fact that I would have to become vulnerable to feel and dwell in the security of God's Love. I would have to let the drawbridge down over the moat for Love to come in.

I also resented the fact that my pursuit made me feel helpless! I felt ashamed of my helplessness and tried to keep it a secret. This reinforced my "masking" behavior and at times allowed me to see myself as quite a spectacle. The more I reviewed my journal the more I saw myself as an emotional indigent—as a poor soul wearing a brand new, intricately beaded designer wedding gown while eating from a trash dumpster on a busy street corner. This perception reinforced my feeling of shame. It was a cruel cycle.

As I continued organizing my entries, I could see that for years the masks won every skirmish and left my heart wounded. The eye-opener for me was to see myself stripped of the masks. I had become so used to wearing them that I nearly lost all awareness that I had them on at all. They had become such a part of me.

At times I grew so battle-weary that I tried to force peace by deciding to accept the conflict as part of my life and embrace it. Thanks be to God that approach never worked because God loved me too much to allow His Spirit in me to embrace such a tormented existence. But neither did He snap His fingers to extinguish the darkness and turn on the lights.

At the time, I thought God hated me because He didn't just snap the lights on or allow me to manage the darkness with my own strategy of coping and acceptance. Back then I thought He showed Love only through instantly snapping on the lights or letting me work it out and cope my way. I knew He was able to grant either, but I also knew that He was not doing it for me. It pained me not to know why.

The fact that God did not grant my request either to turn on the lights or to let me cope really did a number on my head because I could not intellectually process His logic. I understood I was a Christian and that He loved me. I knew He gave His only Son for me. I knew He died for my sins but I wanted to feel His arms wrapped around me. I understood that being a Christian made me a joint heir with Jesus. Yet in spite of what I knew in my head, in my heart I felt like a bastard! I wanted to feel His embrace, His covering, and His care for me. I longed to feel the Love of God and to dwell in its security. *Was that selfish? Was my wanting more than an intellectual assent a sign of ungratefulness in light of all He had already done for me on Calvary?* I wanted more.

Oh how I desperately longed to feel True Love. I felt rejected, abandoned, and disappointed. But can you really get to know someone intimately at the snap of a finger? I had to learn the hard way that the answer was "No." It takes walking together for a measure of time, through it all. It is a process...a *journey*.

God knows my life apart from intimately knowing Him is a life not lived to its fullest. God also knows that it is only in conflict that He will find me consistently rolling out the red carpet for Him to take up residence in my heart.

I allowed Him to take my hand in His and begin to sort out the "issues" of this war raging inside of me. The word "issues" is used often these days to describe the stagnant state of a person's practical development. When we see someone in this state, we think: "He has some issues." I spell and define it the following way: *Ish-you's—imagined state (or status) hampering you*. I had many.

It is always best to start researching an *ish-you* at the root cause, at the beginning. So I had to discover where these masks came from. Why was I so afraid of being emotionally vulnerable? What did I believe so strongly that I needed protection from? Were all of these *ish-you's* a result of my foolish pride or my need to protect already grossly-infected emotional wounds from further injury? It was difficult to find the answers early on, and as a result I was not free to disrobe in the presence of the only One who needed me to so that He could satisfy my heart's longing and quench its most profound need.

> *"Then you will know the truth, and the truth will set you free."*
>
> *(John 8:32 NIV)*

Acknowledging and speaking the truth was the most effective weapon in this high-stakes battle of hide-and-seek I was engaged in. Journaling provided an honest outlet for me and allowed Light to pierce my darkness. The more honest I was to God about my blindness, confusion, and pain, the better able was I to receive more of the Light.

The truth was, I didn't have to wear those masks at all. I had a place I could leave those burdens. I didn't have to exhaust myself trying to figure out which one to wear. Nor did I have to wear myself out shopping for new ones to don.

I had a True Love pleading for me to give Him everything that caused me pain and fear. He wanted them! It was His pleasure to take my burdens!

As I mustered the courage to take the first steps along each pathway of discovery, clarity, and healing through the grace and mercy of God, I came to see that my heart—the core of who I am—was so very anemic. As I carefully examined the hopes and hurts of my heart I learned that God could handle and resolve each one. I saw that I didn't know what I didn't know. I didn't need God to snap on the lights…I needed *Him*. Because I was His beloved daughter, He provided for my need. He rebuilt me from the inside out and did not shortcut the process by "quick fixing" me. He truly and passionately loved me with all He had. He bankrupted Himself for *me*! Yet His supply remains abundant to meet each and every one of my needs, today and forever. And not just for me, but for you, too.

My hope is that you will discover the truth of God's Love for you if you have not already done so, for God's the truth is:

- God is Love.
- He loves you.
- He loves me.

In this book I am going to share with you my journey to finding God's Love for me! But I encourage you to turn to the appendix in the back of the book and read the story of Jonah. I make a lot of references to Jonah because his story highlighted for me the loving nature of God as He deals with humans who are trying to achieve godly objectives.

My journey to Love was like Jonah's trip to Nineveh in that I discovered a depth of God's Love that was more amazing than I had ever imagined!

> *"For this reason I kneel before the Father, from whom his whole family in heaven and on earth derives its name. I pray that out of his glorious riches he may strengthen you with power through his Spirit in your inner being, so that Christ may dwell in your hearts through faith. And I pray that you, being rooted and established in love, may have power, together with all the saints, to grasp how wide and long and high and deep is the love of Christ, and to know this love that surpasses knowledge—that you may be filled to the measure of all the fullness of God."*
>
> *(Ephesians 3:14-19 NIV)*

CHAPTER 1

What is Love?

He's Calling

In my first marriage, I spent myself trying to earn and be found worthy of God's Love. I could not believe that it was available for the asking. So I toiled away in pain trying to earn it by sacrificing my self-will to others, believing this was the price God required me to pay in order to receive and dwell securely in His Love.

A Delicate Petal

"Hey," was the half-hearted greeting offered to me.

I was more hurt than angered by this salute because I was still in the hospital after giving birth to our third child less than 24 hours before.

"So, did they bring the papers down yet?" he asked, a bit sarcastically.

"Yes," I answered.

"What did you name her?"

I responded somewhat sheepishly with a joke, and he cursed me bitterly for nearly half an hour and broke for a couple of minutes only when the nurse took my newborn to have her picture and an ink impression of her hands and feet taken.

For years it had been *my* responsibility to make things happy and calm—or so I believed. The success of our marriage and family life hinged on my ability to accommodate and cope with his extreme emotional instability—or so I thought.

The problem was, I was too often unable to tell where the emotional mines were hidden. I eventually grew tired of tip-toeing around one cautious step after another to avoid setting off an explosion.

I had been accustomed to measured communication, and primarily used open-ended questioning. I had lost—or better said, *abdicated*—my right to question him directly about anything. This indirect method of communication seemed to appease him and prevent a volatile verbal outburst.

The event in the hospital, though, altered me in a way that no other negative exchange had before. My baby daughter was so precious to me, so soft and tiny. My baby girl! The emotional trauma that resulted from this verbal assault as I lay there on the gurney made me feel as though I had been divested of the right to ever expect her to call me her "Mommy." It was as though she had been snatched right out of my arms and given to some other woman with greater, stronger means to raise her. I was too impoverished to raise her well.

Ultimately, she was given to another woman—one who was empowered to rear the infant girl into the prosperous God-fearing woman she was meant to be, a woman to be reckoned with and not denied what was rightfully hers, a woman emanating inner strength that comes only from an accurate knowledge of herself, through the eyes of God, a woman awesome because of her healthy, deep union with God.

But that woman lying there on the hospital gurney, silent against the abusive berating and hushed into a silent stupor, was not such a nurturer for the delicate petal! As the barrage continued, I looked over at the completed forms bearing the name he wanted for her. This time I was too weak to appease the shaming, rageful assault by trying to reason with him. For once, the challenge to turn this negative into a positive defeated me. Self-talk and positive thinking failed, seemingly, for the first time. The task set before me on that gurney was just too great, well beyond my abilities. I was too weary to understand his overreaction to my sheepish joking around. So I rolled off the gurney and waddled to the bathroom with bitter hot tears streaming down my face…as they so often had.

I wasn't just hurt from the emotional ripping but was angry because I could not reason with him to avoid this mistreatment. I was humiliated and ashamed that this was the man who was charged with covering and caring for me. *Wasn't he?*

I wondered if any of the people from our community who were dropping by the hospital to celebrate the new addition to the family overheard any of his cruel outburst. Is that what I had been unable to identify in their fixed stares at me? Did they know the shame of the truth behind our closed doors?

I began to shake uncontrollably. I was simply overwhelmed.

"Lord help me," is all I could whisper in my heart.

There in that bathroom, for the first time in a long time, in the midst of all the boisterous circus-like atmosphere, I allowed myself to connect to the innermost part of me. The truest, deepest part: my heart. My typical "programmed" response to such verbal assaults would be to try to appear healthy and deliver a calm and gentle passive response, all the while silently clinging to the desperate hope of appeasing him and bringing an end to his verbal and emotional battery. In other words, I would put on a mask.

Knowing that my two-year-old son and 16-month-old daughter would soon be there to meet their new baby sister, I mustered enough strength to "pull myself together" and not "crack-up" with the reviving help of meditating on the lyrics of an old gospel song: *Your Grace and Mercy*.

As I stood in the shower, the warm water was more than soothing medicine as I continued to meditate on *Your Grace and Mercy* and tried to let the water's ministry continue to take effect. My labor and delivery nurse was in there with me as I showered based on my medical history, but she gave me an extra measure of care that disquieted my meditation. On this day of my little Petal's birth, the church we attended was the focus of a feature story on the front page of the *Community* section of the most widely distributed newspaper in our home state.

Interviewing for the article had been going on for about a year, and finally the story was in print with the picture of the man I was married to—the church's senior pastor—right there on the front page…just hours before my daughter was born.

The nurse attending to me was of a different faith than I, but she felt comfortable enough to interview me about what life was like as an evangelical Christian, but she was much more interested in probing about what it was like being married to a Senior Pastor. *Wild!*

The lyrics to that old hymn interfered with my efforts to answer her queries graciously:

> *Your grace and mercy*
> *Have brought me through*
> *I'm living this moment*
> *Because of You*
> *I just want to thank you*
> *And praise you too*

Your grace and mercy
   Have brought me through.

My heart began to long and cry in agony, tormented by the mental acrobatics: dismissing the possibility of more cursing waiting for me outside the bathroom door; glossing over the emotional hemorrhaging from the abusive berating while smack dab in the middle of a ministry opportunity; preparing myself for the arrival of my toddlers who were on the way; dodging the judgmental eyes of the public...triage...my body had just delivered a baby!

It was like a countdown to a volcano inside of me. Between my brief answers to the extremely inquisitive nurse, I put my head under the shower water as if to hide from the cruel ferociousness of my mental struggle. During those moments I was more aware than ever before that it was God alone who was keeping me from succumbing to mental madness.

The pressure of my allegiance to keeping on the "Lady Grace" preacher's wife mask nearly made me become unglued. I believed I had to keep it all together. The attention I would have garnered from a melt-down just then would have cost too much! In hindsight, I should have unmasked and trusted God with whatever the consequences resulted from my doing so.

But back to that song that wouldn't "go away," which just then was reduced to just one word: *Mercy*. I could not reconcile that attribute of God to my life right then and the pain and confusion struck my heart deeply. As I caught sight of myself in the bathroom mirror after my shower I didn't recognize the woman staring back at me. It frightened me. I didn't know why or even how I got to this "comatose-like" state. I knew I was alive on the inside, but I had so internalized the constant messages hurled at me that told me I was useless that vitality no longer shone through my eyes. I looked like I had a mask on and it prompted me to probe for answers.

How had one human being gained such power over me, and how on earth had I allowed my own standards to be breached so greatly? My heart cried out: "God, why didn't You spare me? Aren't I living righteously enough to deserve Your merciful protection from him? What is this man's problem anyway? It wasn't supposed to be this way! He is a Christian! A Minister! A Senior Pastor to many families!" How could I have seen this coming? I would have done something if I had seen it coming. Wouldn't I have? Should I go ahead and divorce him? Or was the answer to leave and just separate from him? I wasn't prepared to answer these questions in that bathroom mirror, but what I did was spring a leak.

"I despise my life!"

Finally, truth seeped out from behind my masks! I couldn't believe that I admitted how I truly felt to myself, out loud, without fear! It was an important first step on the journey to Love.

This hospital event was an overload that caused my heart to spring a leak of truth barely the size of a pinhole (although it felt like a deluge). I was afraid that I was too weak to keep it dammed up and prevent a great burst! That pinhole let off enough pressure to keep it from destroying me physically and emotionally. It didn't burst; it seeped. It wasn't loud; it whispered. But at the time it seemed so great a deluge!

God truly knew all about my longing heart's desire to feel His Love and to dwell daily confident in its security. He invited me to walk with Him on a journey that would lead me to the destination of discovering His True Love for me. That moment of truth in the mirror made way for my heart to clearly hear God's call to Love. It wasn't, "Janeen, do/don't get a divorce." It was,

"Janeen, will you let Me care for you?" My bondage and darkness was not about my marriage to him; it was about me.

In order to let God care for me, I would have to hand it all over to Him. *Everything!* But how could I begin to unearth and sort through the years of denial and shame to discover what my true *ish-you's* were—let alone hand it all over to Him? But as that woman in the hospital mirror looked back at me, I took another step: **Confession.**

"I don't know who I am anymore. I feel like I am buried under piles upon piles of stuff. I need help digging out. I've gotta unload this whole heaping mess before it crushes me."

The thought of unearthing and sorting was frightening. I had become so used to covering with the masks. *When did I put those things on anyway? Would others laugh me to scorn when they saw what lay underneath the masks? Would I be accepted and loved by others? Would I be accepted and loved by me?*

I pondered these questions and vacillated between uncovering or staying hidden. I remained stuck for a couple of years, frozen from those moments captured in the hospital mirror trying to decide if I truly wanted to seek out the answers to my questions.

I would have to learn how to dig to the very depths where the true me lived and discover how to live transparently. It was buried way down, much deeper than I thought I was. But I would have to dig down there to find the root cause of my internal conflict: The darkness.

One thing was certain. God already knew the whole truth about me even though I tried so hard to deny and hide it. I had not pulled the masks over His eyes (as I had over my own in many ways), and I needed Him to navigate me out of the blindness the masks caused me.

"Remain in me, and I will remain in you. No branch
can bear fruit by itself; it must remain in the vine.
Neither can you bear fruit unless you remain in me. I
am the vine; you are the branches. If a man remains in
me and I in him, he will bear much fruit; apart from
me you can do nothing. If anyone does not remain in
me, he is like a branch that is thrown away and
withers; such branches are picked up, thrown into the
fire and burned. If you remain in me and my words
remain in you, ask whatever you wish, and it will be
given you. This is to my Father's glory, that you bear
much fruit, showing yourselves to be my disciples."

(John 15:4-8 NIV)

The answers to my questions began to come. The earliest
one, most vivid to me, was the reason God did not spare me from
having to experience this hospital event: He allowed it because
He was being merciful and loving toward me. How? God was encouraging me to fly, to take flight in Him. Indeed, the *pain* and
struggle in my life was intended for more than just the sake of
pain and *struggle*.

"...like an eagle that stirs up its nest
and hovers over its young,
that spreads its wings to catch them
and carries them on its pinions."

(Deuteronomy 32:11 NIV)

In her book *Loving and Letting Go*, Carol Kuykendall's passage on child-rearing aptly applies to how God reared me. She
writes:

"Letting go is a two-part process for the eagle mothers.
First they 'stir up' the nest, making it less comfortable by

removing layers of soft materials to reveal sharp prickly twigs that encourage the eaglet to test its wings.

"Then the parent eagle begins a time of training, standing by during those test flights, fluttering over its young, spreading out its wings, catching the eaglet when it falls, patiently correcting, teaching, and encouraging it to try again. Finally, when the eaglet is capable, it flies away, strong and free and alone, ready and able to seek its potential in life because of the training it received."

Although God never "leaves" me, He let me go through the maturation process so that I could fulfill my purpose and destiny in this life. Being willing, He taught me how to skillfully employ all that I constantly learned and received at His feet.

Greater still, God was discomfiting the nest to encourage me to venture outside of my comfort zone where I could discover His Love for me. I can be stubborn about moving when I am comfortable, especially when nestled in the layers of my soft bedding after a warm luxurious bubble bath. I was too "comfortable" in this nest, and He would eventually have to allow it to become unbearable.

Bout Time

Well there I sat on the floor of our family room exhausted from the rigors of the day as a homemaker and mom of three toddlers, now ages two, three, and four years old. I was bursting with a sense of excitement that I could not quite explain. It was as if a cool breeze had blown across my hot face and managed to clear away a veil of dimness in my eyes.

The pinhole of light that shined through at the hospital two years before had become a beam growing inside me. The breach in the dam was bigger now and the sound of the pressure being let off was louder and the flow greater as it washed up the debris.

The house had been looking like a fortified demonic stronghold pretty consistently over the years, especially in the kitchen and laundry departments. I could not remember the last time there had been a drawer full of clean silverware or a dresser full of clean underwear. There were more Sundays he stood before the congregation delivering the sermon in swim trunks underneath his drycleaned designer suit than I would care to recall.

But this day, as I sat there on the floor of the family room, I was so tired of the mess that I was determined that my home would be in this shape NO LONGER! It was about 8:30 p.m. and I began cleaning the house from top to bottom with zest and zeal. An unmistakable newness was looming in the air (not just from the air freshener's fresh, clean scent). It was strange: After determining in my heart to get this menial task completed, I could almost touch this Ominous Presence that was wooing me along from one room of the house to the next. My energy level and passion to get it all done was positively supernatural! I cleaned the house from top to bottom before, but this time it was somehow markedly different.

Between sinkfuls of washed dishes I would throw another load of dirty clothes in the washer, and throw out a moldy pile (as a result of excess laundry being thrown onto the basement floor, which frequently flooded), then fold up what was left of the freshly cleaned, fresh smelling ones.

Instead of vacuuming the carpeted two-story parsonage we called home, I swept the floors with a broom so as not to awaken everyone in the house.

I finally finished the cleaning at about 3:00 a.m. It was all picked up, spic and span. Even though I knew my youngest child would be awakening shortly and the day would dawn and tap what little energy I had left, I felt rested and energized. *Free!* I felt like throwing a party. So I did the unthinkable. I threw Luther Vandross on the CD player and swayed to the music. It was wonderful.

While there were well over 300 gospel CDs and about 20 secular CDs in our house, I had not selected and played a CD in our home for years! Something so simple had eluded me all of this time and a tear streamed down my cheek as I realized it. It also dawned on me that I had not opened the mail or answered the phone or the door in a long time either. This moment was rich beyond description.

Instantly, layers of bondage that had barred me from such basic personal freedoms fell away and renewed courage took its place. I reconnected with a part of my heart that had been, for all intents and purposes, *dead*. I had become aware of myself, much like a baby who is entertained by the sound of her very own giggle. Suddenly and oddly, I got tickled silly, too.

Just as I was drifting down memory lane with Luther Vandross' greatest hits, I heard a jarring BUZZZZZ! I had forgotten all about that last load of clothes in the dryer. But I tell you that though the dryer signal startled me, the sounds of liberty's bells rang out over it. As a matter of fact, as I was nearing the end of folding that last load of laundry, that bell was ringing so loudly it awakened him!

As the door to the den flung open, the gale force wind of negative emotions and bitter words were stirred against my back once again. This time my heart and mind transcended the torrent through His Spirit.

> *"It is for freedom that Christ has set us free. Stand firm,*
> *then, and do not let yourselves be burdened again by a*
> *yoke of slavery."*
>
> *(Galatians 5:1 NIV)*

I exercised my freedom and chose no longer to accept the neglect and filth of the house. I exercised freedom to indulge in a little pleasure enjoying my musical selection. Overall I felt confident and capable again to exercise the desire of my will in my marital relationship. I stood up and planted in my resolve to stand. As the weak, I declared I was strong. In my courage I could feel the warmth of His Spirit and it felt good.

Layers of bondage had definitely fallen away to the point that I could see greater cords and shackles flailing in the winds all around me. There were some that were still strongly bolted down to the deck of this rickety relation-*ship*.

What were the cords and shackles made of that enabled them to hold so fast and who put them there?

As I asked God to unmask the spiritual villains, I could sense God ushering me down a new pathway. This rickety ship with tattered sails found me in uncharted waters sailing as I had for years with no compass.

God wanted to answer my questions, but even more He wanted to create an atmosphere that would lead me to set my sails to His wind and draw eagerly closer and more intimately toward Him.

Lady Grace

Fresh off winning that bout, this mountaintop experience gave me a new view of my surroundings. In addition to those bolted down shackles, I saw that I had options that I wouldn't have acknowledged—let alone exercised—before.

It had been over six months since I had ventured beyond the driveway of our home—mainly because we lived in the church parsonage and the only time I got away from the house was when I walked next door to the church on Sundays. During this period, he did all the grocery shopping and ran all of the errands for the household.

I had become isolated from the world, and the high walls of the parsonage were nearly impenetrable. His three Rottweilers patrolling the perimeter contributed to this, but the real reason for the isolation was that after the church deeded the parsonage over to him, and it became *his* house, the glass walls became steel.

As the "pastor's wife," for years I had sat alone on the front row. As attendees filed out of the church at the close of the service, I would often stand by his side at the back door and see them out—smiling, hugging, encouraging, and laughing all the while...*alone.*

Most of my attempts to have a personal relationship with "the girls" in the congregation were foiled by their inability to see me separate from the pastor. One lady in the church told me, "If I went with you to the mall I would feel like I was shopping for lingerie with "The Pastor."

Initially I was hurt but over time it turned to bitterness. It took time to resolve that bitterness, too. I accepted "their way" of relating to me and enabled their thinking by putting on my "Lady Grace" preacher's wife mask.

My upbringing fostered the idea of church members being an extended family. This was absolutely *not* the perspective of the parishioners in my new hometown. We were in a New England state with a large Roman Catholic presence; fewer than two in a hundred were evangelical Christians. The traditions some held onto made for a tough social transition when they joined our non-denominational, Baptist-affiliated church.

At times I would see them struggling between "father" and "pastor" when they were addressing him. So, as you might imagine, those members definitely could not bring themselves to see me as "one of the girls." They were too busy processing and coming to terms with their feelings of illegitimacy regarding their "pastor" being married.

Then there were the members who were new to church life altogether. Sometimes all the "professional" churchgoers made them so uncomfortable that they didn't know whether to bow, bend, or make direct eye contact to address me in an "acceptable" manner.

As they saw me providing administrative support and teaching in the women's, children's, and music ministry they must have concluded that I was simply a "helpmate suitable." They just couldn't seem to loosen up enough, though, to see me as one of "the girls."

Shopping for the Free Indeed

Enough truth was shining in my heart to allow me to see enough firm ground in front of my foot to venture taking another step forward. The parsonage walls were coming down...or at least the drawbridge over the moat. For starters I was leaving the driveway! To the grocery store! Unaccompanied!

In preparation for my *grand junk food acquisition*, I had to pull out an old checkbook of mine to study it. I had worked at a bank before, but it had been so long since I had written a check, or even seen one, that I had forgotten how. It had been so long, in fact, that I wondered if my account had been subjected to escheatment.

I called the bank to get a status on my account. Just as I had anticipated, a previous coworker, from years earlier, answered my call. I must admit that on that day I was finally able to appreciate her abrupt style for placing customers on hold and passing the call along to a greener employee for servicing.

At the store I took my time selecting my items, but what I remember most was the near debilitating feelings of insecurity I had at the checkout counter. When it was time to write the check to pay for my items, I felt so sick. I was visibly nervous because I had become so conditioned by the years of extreme manipulation.... Money for a trip to the beauty parlor taken away minutes before my scheduled appointment to teach me a "lesson"; keys to the car and house secretly removed from my key chain to leverage his demand for his terms to be met.... All that made this simple transaction at the grocery store a bondage breaker. It was a tough nut to crack!

I was so fidgety that the cashier called the manager over for verification of the check, which made me even more fidgety. The check was only a little over $3.00! I wanted to run, but I prayerfully fought the urge and planted myself in my resolve to stand. The following verse echoed from the night before.

> *"It is for freedom that Christ has set us free. Stand firm, then, and do not let yourselves be burdened again by a yoke of slavery."*
>
> *(Galatians 5:1 NIV)*

I had successfully made the purchase and I couldn't help but giggle as I reclined in my car and took a bite from my candy bar and saddled up for the ride home. It was a trip! I was near manic as I constantly checked and readjusted my mirrors to insure that I wasn't displeasing any drivers around me with my speed or lane choice.

I passed the turn onto the street where I lived twice! The first time was because I didn't want to anger the car approaching in my turn lane. I really didn't want any confrontation with him by making him think I was "cutting him off" at the pass by moving into his lane too abruptly. So I did not exercise my right and allow myself to choose to signal and change lanes. Instead, I let his convenience take precedence over my incredible *inconvenience*. I thought this was the behavior God required. I thought this was humility. I thought God would be pleased with me and affirm by flooding my heart with His Love and presence.

The second time was when I nearly caused an accident trying desperately to avoid a confrontation with another driver. He was bulling his way out of a side street illegally, and I held up traffic at the major intersection to assist him, which succeeded in making everyone behind me very mad at me!

In my effort to lag far enough behind to avoid all those drivers I had upset, I sped past my street for the second time. I drove down a half a mile and took refuge in a library parking lot for about 10 minutes and thought about it: Those other drivers clearly disagreed with my commitment to sacrifice my self-will for another. My avoidance of confrontation was dangerous to me and to them.

But I finally arrived home safely, though I was clearly shaken. I dragged all of my strewed emotions in the door and quietly settled my body in the chair at the table.

Victory.

As I sat there sipping my soda and chomping on my chips, I began to reflect and examine my heart about the events of the day, which started before I jumped in the "getaway" car.

I had answered the phone before I left for the store, amidst the major conflict that was stirring up, and also intercepted the mail and sorted it while pointing direct questions about some of the senders. This was no easy task considering that at some point in my spiritual development I was poisoned by toxic theology —which is sort of like bad seafood—especially with the misinterpretation of the following verse:

> *"Do nothing out of selfish ambition or vain conceit, but in humility consider others better than yourselves."*
> *(Philippians 2:3 NIV)*

I desired to feel God's loving presence in my heart everyday and dwell in the security of knowing He was ever with me. I thought that the price I had to pay to earn this and prove I was worthy to receive it was sacrificing my self-will to others. I understood that self-sacrifice was the demonstration of humility (Philippians 2:1-4). This misunderstanding—thinking that self-sacrifice would merit God's loving presence—amounted to heresy because it was devoid of godly boundaries and it was nurtured further in my unhealthy marital relationship.

Before I understood what godly boundaries were and how to apply them in my life, I approached my unhealthy marriage as an opportunity to earn and prove my worthiness to God. What I really needed to do was draw closer to Him and recognize that through salvation He was already near me. It was still too dark for me to see this.

Those potato chips were good as I smacked and crunched like a kid with no table manners. My childlike freedom didn't jibe with the "Lady Grace" mask I wore, so I took it off and put it down near me. Besides, being outside exposed me to the Sonshine again, and the heat made wearing that heavy thing too uncomfortable.

The "Do-Bot" Thing!

I married at 19 years old to the "strong silent type." I wished that I had a man in my daily life who loved me enough to wisely press my finance's buttons and skillfully stir up his deep waters to expose what lay beneath.

In their book *The Two Sides of Love*, Gary Smalley and John Trent describe in great detail human temperament strengths and weaknesses by dividing them into four major categories. While mostly everyone has a mixture of the four one is typically dominant. They write:

"(Golden Retrievers) are just like their counterparts in nature. If you could pick one word to describe them, it would be loyalty. They're so loyal, in fact, that they can absorb the most emotional pain and punishment in relationships—and still stay committed. They're great listeners, empathizers and warm encouragers—all strong softside skills. But they tend to be such pleasers that they can have great difficulty in adding the hard side of love when it's needed."

My dominant bent is toward the "Golden Retriever" temperament. God gave me my temperament just as He gave you yours. The invitation I make for His Spirit to direct my life allows God to keep the dominant from destroying me. God is the equalizer and stabilizing force. I have to lean on God moment by moment to achieve optimum results in managing my temperament. If not, I expose myself to awful bouts of pain as I trip and fall from the predisposed top heaviness.

I was so out of God's control and under others' control because I was leaning on my own understanding. I wound up doing things I did not want to do and receiving the opposite of what I wanted.

> *"Trust in the Lord with all your heart and lean not on*
> *your own understanding; in all your ways acknowl-*
> *edge him, and he will make your paths straight."*
> *(Proverbs 3:5-6 NIV)*

The price tag on proving and earning my worthiness to receive and feel God's loving presence was far higher than I could
afford. My attempt to secure it apart from trusting in the finished
work of the cross caused my own self-abuse. I became a "do-bot."

A robot is an inanimate machine that mimics the behavior of
a sentient (or thinking) being. The one who has the robot's re-
mote control has absolute power over its operation. A "do-bot" is
a sentient being that mimics the behavior of a robot. The brazen
who are allowed to control it have power over its operation.

All the circus noise I allowed in my life due to my lack of
boundaries contributed to my blindness and abuse. No matter
how hard I tried to stop being a "do-bot," I simply couldn't. I kept
repeating the same behavior. God wanted to silence the noise
and heal me but to do so He needed to redirect my focus towards
an intimate relationship with Him. For my part, I would have to
allow Him to.

I realized eventually that God's wisdom to make choices and
to choose better had been available for me to use all along. All I
had to do was ask the One who gives it liberally (James 1:5). It
was not selfish and wrong to use the brain God gave me and exe-
cute my choices. Neither was it wrong to ask for God's help with
what I didn't know. It was absolutely appropriate to be honest
and truthful at the expense of unity. My longing to feel the envel-
oping presence of God's Love and dwell in the security of knowing that He was ever near me was not only okay but a normal
part of His design for my life. Acknowledging that need and pur-

suing its remedy was not weakness as I once thought. Rather, it was the beginning of understanding.

> *"The fear of the LORD is the beginning of wisdom, and*
> *knowledge of the Holy One is understanding."*
>
> *(Proverbs 9:10 NIV)*

As I sat there at the table finishing up my junk food feast, I quietly pondered my marriage. Though my heart's will was getting stronger it needed a heavy dose of Godly boundaries and "tough love." I needed to separate from him, but all those years during which my self-worth eroded left me afraid to make the change.

My fear was bigger than the God I claimed to believe in! Though I knew He created the world, I made decisions as though He was incapable of caring for the material needs of my children and me. Intellectually, I knew the facts about the marvelous exploits performed by the God of the Bible I professed to believe in, but my low self-worth impeded the Bible's ability to become practical revelation in my life. So instead of asking for His help and "inconveniencing" Him with a request from "little old me," I welded a mighty steel chin on my "strong and tough" mask.

All seemed well for a short while, and that steel-chinned strong and tough mask held up through a lot, until one day.... *Crack!*

CHAPTER 2

Bound for Love

Answer the Call?

Early on in my journey, I wanted to blame people for my darkness—my belief that God didn't love me. I could not fully understand that I would feel the Love I longed for *only through an intimate relationship with Him*. I could identify that the sacrifice of my self-will to others was a failed formula, yet I still put *people* in my God-loves-me equation. I believed that the needs of my heart should have been met in relationships with certain people. This led me to place unrealistic expectations on myself and others to get this need met. Unfortunately, this approach still placed the wellness of my heart's condition at their whim.

While I experienced a degree of heartwarming fulfillment when someone found pleasure in me, it didn't come close to meeting my deepest and most critical need to feel Loved. I couldn't comprehend God's grace: that He *already* loved me to the max! To be honest, one of the main reasons I could not comprehend this loving grace was that I was afraid to hope it was true…and thus I relegated myself to trust in my own worthiness and not in His. How cruel it was to believe that I could make myself worthy of God's Love.

This long pathway taught me that my only hope of getting my longing heart's need met from God was to release what I had obligated others to do for me. I had to release me, too. I had to own this releasing! But as I went about trying to release this human dimension of being worthy of God's Love, a few more problems in my approach arose. For one, as my doubts about His ability to care for me began to surface and I made certain choices to earn others' care, it was a clear reflection in my belief that God was not only too small but untrustworthy to meet my needs. Second, I had this notion of God as a *preoccupied parent*, and this precipitated more self-abuse as I tried to take ownership of getting Him to draw nearer to me outside the context of an intimate relationship.

In chapter one I shared a few stories that exposed my belief that God was too small and untrustworthy. My perception that God was a preoccupied parent manifested in a peculiar behavior pattern as I attempted to draw out His compassion and presence—much like a child who will act out to get the attention of a preoccupied human parent.

I related to God much like a baby who purposefully falls down to draw out the compassionate care of her parent. The tiny cute person is pretty skillful in working her plan because typically someone who hears the *cutie* go *splat* on the ground will drop everything for a moment and attend to the baby's needs. A child may purposefully fall down or vomit or even run straight into harm's way consciously (sometimes even at the expense of an injury) to get the parent to draw near to them.

I, too, kept falling down subconsciously to keep the gentle compassionate presence of God near me. I did feel His Love, but only one aspect of it. Seeking his loving attention this way was the extent (the boundary) of relational capacity I opened myself up to receive from Him. It provided an emotional "quick fix."

God is close to the brokenhearted (Psalm 34:18), and indeed I felt Him close to me in a "weepy" kind of way. My Heavenly Father had more than bandages for my scrapes, an ice pack for my bruises, and pity for my injuries. He wanted to teach me how to walk, run, soar, and keep from ever falling down.

In the Garden

After consulting with two psychologists and one Christian marriage and family counselor over a three-year period, we were left with the conclusion that he was suffering from chronic depression. Each of the professionals believed that it stemmed largely from *ish-you's* in his childhood that apparently began to manifest in chronic depression during the second year of our marriage.

In our marriage counseling sessions, the therapists typically noted within the first hour that I was withstanding a considerable amount of emotional abuse. They advised me to take some measures to consider my own psychological health, to which he responded in fury. Needless to say, each of these attempts at counseling was cut short, too.

I had endured a lot of neglect and mistreatment, which contributed to the erosion of my self-worth. The verbal abuse and mind games had gotten so bad that I did things to avoid the conflict that ended up further enabling his unhealthy behavior towards me.

I made maxi-pads and diapers out of tissue and packing tape. I had panty hose with so much clear nail polish on them it's a wonder the friction didn't set on fire the church pew I sat on. My toothbrush looked like a piece of chewed sugar cane. But I accepted all of this. I endured it as a good soldier at war. At the time, the only booty I wanted was a garden. I did all the yard work anyway, so it shouldn't have been that big a deal to get some support to make this happen.

I enjoy the outdoors tremendously and looked forward to planting a garden with my children. My mom and grandma had gardens. I had so many cherished memories and learned so many life-lessons gardening I wanted to share them with my children as well. So let the gardening begin!

It took a week to prepare the soil of our plot, and planting seeds took a while because the children had a passion to *pick* the fruit. They were so excited, and so was I. A few weeks later, after weeding, watering, and watching, the first fruits of our labor appeared.

Our garden did so well it inspired a few ladies in the church to plant one of their own. It was bountiful and made more than enough tomatoes, cucumbers, and green beans, so we were able to share.

One evening, as was typical, he assured me (as usual) that he had put the three Rottweilers he owned away. Contrary to what he said, though, he usually left them uncaged to roam around unsupervised. I would hear them running around and get out of bed to put them away to keep some semblance of order in the yard. On this particular night I was too exhausted from the rigors of the day and fell asleep. To my horror, when I got up in the morning I discovered that the entire garden was dug up...destroyed!

I was crushed! We had had many close calls like this before, and knowing the degree of dysfunction and unhealthiness in our relationship I should have known better than to expect any other outcome. Yet I kept putting myself in harm's way expecting a different outcome. I felt as though God owed me protection in the midst of this on account of the effort I put forth to achieve such a bountiful garden...and all the righteous fruit it was bearing in the quality of life for the children...and how it was inspiring the other ladies in the church.

The Damsel In Distress—Bad Fairy Tale

I developed some terrible habits of setting myself up in humiliating situations to force his hand to keep feeding my heart crumbs of compassion and understanding. Using my own righteous behavior as a tool to secure it only succeeded in setting me up for anguish, as I could not logically reconcile the outcome. Though my sweat-and-tears efforts forced his *head* from time to time, it never forced his *heart*. Only the Spirit of God can do that. Besides, only God could reach my heart to the depth I needed.

> *"The king's heart is in the hand of the LORD;*
> *he directs it like a watercourse wherever he pleases."*
> *(Proverbs 21:1 NIV)*

From time to time he would quote that scripture about "wives be submissive," and I shut my eyes, ears, and heart to the other part of that same passage of scripture that admonished "husbands to love their wives as Christ loved the church and gave himself for it" (Ephesians 5:21-25). I didn't bring that up because I wanted to avoid confrontation. Though it appeared passive, my pursuit was aggressively reckless, and I threw my white silk lace handkerchief on the floor in an effort to get him to meet my longing heart's needs. Though as my husband he was supposed to meet some of my needs, he was simply not designed to meet those most critical needs. I had ignorantly lumped it all into one need and expected God to provide for it through him.

We invited a ministering couple to dine at our house. They were about 30 or 40 years older than I. They graciously accepted the invitation several weeks before and were driving about 60 miles from a neighboring city in Massachusetts. I must admit that I felt a little pressure, given their years in the ministry, to exhibit proper etiquette and good old-fashioned manners. I wasn't going to put that "Lady Grace" mask on again though. I was going to genuinely serve them as was my heart's desire.

A short time before they arrived, the countertops were still piled high with dishes. It looked as if we were packing up and moving out. The plan was to emerge with a clean dignified personal appearance and a tidy home. Of course, ironing the table linens, setting the table, and fan-folding the napkins was a must. But attempting these simple tasks put me on the fringes. It's not like the children and dogs quietly stayed put in the closet to accommodate my efforts.

And of course he and I were embroiled in a silent war over who would wash the dishes. I was looking for understanding. I thought that if I cooked it was only fair that he be responsible for washing the dishes. I though it, but would not dare say it.

He finally arrived home less than an hour before our guests were due to arrive freshly-shaven, cologned, and clad in new clothes. He quickly surveyed the kitchen in a shambles and my personal appearance and seemed genuinely concerned. I was mapping toward getting some understanding. He wanted to make a good impression on our guests and getting in agreement with me was the consequence. I feasted on the crumb!

So, guess what?

He volunteered to wash the dishes to allow me to make myself presentable. He picked up my hankie off the floor!

Just as I was heading up the stairs to get ready, he asked me a question.

"What do you have planned to serve our guests?"

Being the "delicate damsel" I wanted to pass out. I didn't remember the main thing, *the main thing!*

Our refrigerator was stocked with a partial stalk of semi-wilted celery, half a container of salad dressing, and some dregs of butter. The freezer had one pack of frozen chicken legs. Our shelves had one container of rice, a can of soup, and a couple of jars of seasoning. We also had a candy dish filled with ketchup and soy sauce packets from fast food restaurants. Bottom line, there was no food ready to prepare *and all* of our dishes were dirty.

I was feeling faint (at least I acted like it). I also felt my new hero-volunteer's commitment waning in the face of the myriad tasks that needed to be completed to pull this evening off...and it was to begin in less than an hour.

Like a flash of lightning a brilliant idea popped into my light head: "Let's just take them out to eat?" He was averse to the idea, saying what was the use of inviting them *over* if we really weren't going to have them *over*? Our home would be the perfect setting for the deep, intimate fellowship we desired. No sooner than I agreed, another flash of lightning occurred: He blasted out the door!

"Janeen," he said, "don't stress out about cooking a large dinner. I'll just get some stuff to make a nice large salad."

His attempt at getting in agreement with me was welcome and warmed my heart, but I had pulled out the china (of course they were the only clean dishes in the house) and set a beautiful formal dining table to invite them to drive this far for *SALAD*!

And guess what else the happy, eager shopper didn't do?

Wash those dishes!

I could have sworn that I heard him say, "Uh-oh, sweetie, your hankie dropped" when he volunteered to wash the dishes. But he didn't pick it up off the floor! He got mud all over it when he bolted out the door.

Fifteen minutes before they arrived, I looked just like the kitchen—a stressed mess! I had just lost my volunteer (knight in shining armor) and nothing was cooked! I ran upstairs to rinse what needed to be soaked and powder what needed to be painted. I knew our guests would be on time and that they would be walking into the midst of our crossfire.

What felt like seconds later, I heard a car crunching into our seashell-covered driveway. Back then as you pulled down into the driveway you had a clear view into the kitchen.

I unrealistically hoped it was him returning from the store, but deep down I knew better. In my dash to peak out the corner of the window to confirm my suspicion, I stared straight into the beam of the headlights. It was as though I had just looked directly into the light of the sun. A blast of bright light usually triggers a migraine for me. So as I was half-blinded and stumbling in mild brain-pain, the sound of the doorbell was like fingernails unmercifully raking across a chalkboard. Also, though I could taste it, I couldn't see the white toothpaste on my red lipstick because of the haloes and auras the migraine was bringing on. The time I should have been spending preparing to usher them through the front door, I spent struggling to get that toothpaste glue all off.

But as you might have guessed, our guests unfortunately entered through the kitchen. I was stumbling and fumbling around in such a rushed panic. As I think back on that night, I laugh myself to tears. It must have struck them like something out of a cartoon strip.

I wanted to run out of the front door as they entered through the kitchen door. I couldn't do that, though, because I couldn't just leave them on the kitchen doorstep and pretend no one was at home after they had driven so far to visit.

I answered the kitchen door (in the dark) and greeted them with big hugs. I was apologetic for the kitchen while grinning like something was in my teeth.

About 20 awkward minutes later he walked in.

What a set up!

The damsel in distress routine got me nothing! My hankie was still on the floor, and he was getting more mud on it from his shoe.

I was about to do something to head off this frayed situation. I chose not to.

I could have put my hair up in a ponytail and ordered take out. Those were decisions I was empowered to make. Our guests were so gracious; they just wanted to fellowship. I could have called and canceled our dinner date and they would have understood. Even if they hadn't, I would have understood that my need to be honest was far more important than unity. I also could have washed those dishes myself.

But even more than all that… I should have taken ownership and picked up my hankie *myself*.

The Slap

It was our oldest child's first school play. It was such a precious occasion. The camera and wardrobe were all prepared the night before. Such high hopes for this moment in the life of our family. We had to have him there at the school on time if not a few minutes early to rehearse and prepare for the parents' arrival and his thespian debut.

The baby was up early and needed a bath. I woke up the two older children and got them fed and dressed, as usual. I then cared for my own needs by hurriedly rinsing what needed to be soaked and powdering what needed to be painted. All this was done to ensure that Junior got to the school on time. I ran upstairs to find *him* still in the bed. We needed to be walking out of the door in fewer than 10 minutes even to be "on time" because by now we were too late to be there early. *How could he?* I wondered? *Where's the understanding?*

"Honey, you need to get up," I told him. "Junior is going to be late, and I was hoping we'd get good seats so that he can see us watching him from the audience."

"....Janeen! I'm coming!"

As he finally rolled out of the bed, I began to take the rollers out of my hair: Last thing for me to do.

The children were now ready and waiting at the bottom of the stairs. I gathered my brush and comb to prepare to finish my hair in the car when to my surprise I heard the shower turn on. He was climbing into the shower! I was outraged!

I knocked on the bathroom door and reminded him how late we were...to no avail! I returned to my vanity, feeling as if I were in stocks, the sound of the ticking clock sickening me. He came out of the bathroom before taking his shower and wanted to know why I was making such a big fuss. I remained focused on my purpose; I just hadn't time to spare for an argument.

I suggested that he give me the keys to one of *his* four cars in our driveway so I could drive the children to the school. I promised to save a seat for him, which didn't help. He was adamant in his rejection. That would never do, and besides, he accused, I was trying to embarrass him by attending the event without him.

Again, I tried to keep the conversation focused on the urgent issue—getting Junior to the school on time. That was the priority at hand!

But not for him. He then began to argue in an almost unintelligible gibberish similar to that of a stammering drunk.

By now, the children had turned on cartoons downstairs, and Junior was running late. I was livid! I was hurting for Junior, too. I returned to my vanity and dressing area feeling woeful. He had entered and exited the bathroom again and again, and now we were both screaming at the top of our lungs. I was so angry at feeling caged because the consequence was being felt by my little thespian.

In our house, it was rare that my voice matched the same level and intensity as his. Though now I had begun to test my wings, albeit passively, this was becoming more frequent.

"You are a controlling B*%~#," he screamed at me, and I fired back: "You are a sorry man, you punk." With that, he walked right over to my vanity and dared me to say it again. And I did. At which he repeated "B*%~#" and I countered "Punk," back and forth we exchanged about five times nearly nose to nose and then, *SLAP!* He struck me across the face!

My nest, which had been my security, was now giving way. It wasn't made of twigs and sticks but of my belief that my righteousness would cause God to miraculously rain down fire from heaven and deliver me without me having to ask Him to.

It was frightening to see my works-righteousness in millions of pieces about my feet. I spent myself on doing right to the "letter of the law" and wholly trusted in that to deliver me and "fix" everything. I was hanging on to my nest now as if my life depended on it. I was at war with my own fatigue. But God wasn't going to shove me out. I would have to jump.

By trusting in my own righteousness rather than in God's to secure my deliverance, I created conditions favorable for unhealthiness in that marriage. All I could do and all I was *supposed* to do was accept and embrace the Loving trustworthiness of God.

The Deck on that "Holy-Day"

It was the holiday season and his mother passed away. We flew home to California to bury her and enjoy as best we could the rest of the holidays with our families. As the time drew near for us to return home to New England, he informed me that he would not be returning with the children and me. Mind you, the children and I had flown without him to California for the funeral, too. (Those of you who have traveled with children on an airplane from one coast to another can surely appreciate my buckled knees at the thought of having to do this again.)

We made it to the airport with little money. We had just enough to eat at the fast-food restaurant in the airport as we waited to board our flight. A deacon from the church would be awaiting our arrival to carry us home from the airport.

It always seemed that every time we returned from vacation our basement would be flooded and there would be no heat and no food. This trip I was prepared! I had serviced and cleaned the kerosene heaters, cleaned the sump pump, and purchased groceries and stocked the freezer and the cupboards. I was ready.

To my surprise another member of the church greeted us at the airport—a man *he* bitterly despised because this member and his family were "too nosey."

The man was concerned for us. A cold front had hovered over New England for the past several days and, of course, our house would be freezing cold. The hour was late and it was doubtful that the temperature was habitable. I tried to brush off his concern by highlighting the "good" on our holiday vacation.

As we pulled up to the house it seemed so dark. Not just the kind of darkness no electricity brings…it was like a deep darkness portrayed in horror movies (the only thing missing was a colony of vultures circling). It was about 2:00 a.m. and the children and I were bushed.

The church member waited in the kitchen and remarked on how bitterly cold it was in the house as I checked out the premises, looking forward to giving him the all-clear signal. I assured him that I was prepared for the cold this time and had cleaned the kerosene heaters. But…

As I flipped the switch on the heaters, nothing happened. I also began to notice a weird, unfamiliar odor in the house. He helped me try to start the heater as the children were celebrating their homecoming in the back bedrooms. Their joy distracted my attention from the heaters and that odd odor.

I assured him that we would be just fine. I would turn on the stove and fashion the bed sheet over the kitchen doorway to keep in the heat for warmth. He strongly objected because it was near zero in the house and it would take a long time to get heat from the "clean kitchen" to the children's back bedrooms. Also, he said, he and his wife had made provision for us in the event we needed to stay with them because, as he put it, they just had a *feeling* something like this might happen. He said that he just couldn't stomach leaving us in the house in that condition.

I tried to smile and convince him otherwise and assure him that we would be okay. He conceded, but only on the condition I would promise to call his family if it was too much to bear. I agreed. He reluctantly left, and I called California to let the family know that we had arrived safely.

I mentioned to my sister that there was a strange odor and now some scratching noises I had just begun to hear. I thought that it might be the dogs, seeing as their cage was near the window I was looking out of. But they had never been able to reach from their cages all the way to the windows. My sister asked where the noise was coming and promised to hold the line as I went to investigate. I soon discovered that the basement was severely flooded and that the noises were coming from behind one of our big screen televisions.

RATS!

They were in the walls throughout the house. I thought I would die. I couldn't stand there in disbelief too long, though, because of the children! They were still celebrating in the back rooms. I ran back there, frantic, seeing now the shredded pieces of fabric on the carpet from the nesting rodents, but I quickly composed myself enough to feign a smile and tell them that the kitchen was now warm from the stove heat and that it would be best to huddle in there for a while.

I returned to the phone and shared with my sister all I had discovered. She clicked over for me on her three-way phone line and dialed. As I began to tell *him* the condition of the house his response was, "What do you want me to do about it?" I desperately blurted out, "Well, when are you coming home?" His sharp response was: "I don't know."

"We need help," I squeaked out. "What am I supposed to do?"

"Janeen, I guess you'll just have to figure something out." At that moment an irreversible shift happened in our relationship that changed things between him and me forever.

I had no money, no access to money, and no resources to secure the help we needed. I hung up with my sister and turned to the perky faces of my three grinning babies whose cheeks and noses were now red. I closed my eyes in blind faith, hugged them tight, and jumped from my nest.

Overboard I went into the crashing waves below....

CHAPTER 3

What Love is Not

Overboard...Can't Swim

"You hurled me into the deep,
into the very heart of the seas,
and the currents swirled about me;
all your waves and breakers
swept over me. I said, 'I have been banished
from your sight;
yet I will look again
toward your holy temple.'"

(Jonah 2:3-4 NIV)

AS I STRUGGLED in the crashing waves, slapping at the water, gasping desperately for air, I ingested a lot of sea. The salty water made me a little delirious but also frustrated me because what I thought should have sustained me...*harmed* me.

My will was certainly engaged to finish this marathon swim, but that alone was not enough to teach me how to swim. I needed to learn and apply new skills. I needed to settle on my decision to trust God, quarantine the violations I had experienced, and frame a new perspective and approach to the new life I was now bound for.

All my anxious laboring only added to my fear of embracing all this change. I started to miss my old nest a little and actually still clutched a little piece of twig in my hand. It was so lonely adrift on the vast, dark, storm-ridden sea. In my loneliness and fear I made a surface level appeal to God for His help.

Lesson #1—Trust God? Trust God!

Although I was the same dress size for years, fashion styles had definitely changed. I decided that I would let go and reduce my wardrobe. I read Anne Ortlund's book *Disciplines of a Beautiful Woman,* which helped me understand stewardship with clothing in a whole new light. I followed her advice and got rid of garments that were torn, faded, worn, or outdated—or all of the above. I mean, come on, is it really appropriate to wear a faded taffeta prom dress to run errands? This effort was going to reduce my wardrobe to slim pickin's, but I needed to admit that I needed new clothing.

He always committed to making me look like the toast of the town on Sunday morning for church service, but when the clock struck midnight on Monday morning the gown, slippers, and stage coach turned back to appropriate servant's garb. I had been so used to looking in a closet full of nothing to wear that the thought of not having to stress out doing that anymore was a welcome change.

The benefit of reducing my wardrobe as a matter of practical sense was liberating—it freed me from stress and wasted time. The stress came largely from *his* response to my utterance of the old line: "I have nothing to wear." "Woman," he would say, "you got a whole closet full of clothes. Surely there is something in there for you to wear."

It was a little scary at first because the children were growing like weeds and I did need presentable clothing for running errands in the community. Of course now that leaving the driveway had become a regular part of my life, I was not going to allow something as little as my wardrobe to keep me behind the steel wall. I dared to trust that God was concerned about what concerned me when it came to food, clothing, and shelter. I had felt uncomfortable walking around looking less than my best for far too long. And, besides, when I did run errands it kept me from swimming through my closet full of "nothing to wear."

Maternity clothes, layettes, baby blankets, bottles, monitors, and toys were surrendered. Plastic pumps from the 80s, Sunday hats with bent rims or felt rubbed beyond repair were offered up. No item was too sacred to be hauled off to the local thrift store or out to the trash. Things by the trashbagful got the boot. It was like spring cleaning, complete with that light airy feeling of "newness" afterward. It intoxicated me.

I giggled a lot during the three days it took to complete this thinning task. In spite of the protest and promises that I would "regret it," I trusted God to provide what the children and I needed. I started to act on my belief that God was trustworthy and would faithfully grant requests for the legitimate physical needs of His children.

After I completed the task I lay prostrate in prayer to God, not knowing what to say, thankful but concerned, trusting but insecure: Guess what? The very next morning I received a huge bag of clothes that were not only stylish but *fit* me. Two days later there came a huge bag of clothes that were not only stylish but fit the *children*. God used the Robinson family to bless me and my babies. Who would have imagined that she, too, would feel inclined to do some cleaning of her own and give the items to me? She and I were the same size. She also had children who were growing like weeds so I had "choice pickin's" for my own.

In the wake of this unmistakable display of God's power to reward openly those who seek Him in secret I felt like superwoman. I had tapped into the heart of God. I stepped out in faith and trusted Him to properly conclude the matter. Somehow I would have to learn how to hone the practice of prayer.

Lesson #2—Acceptance

In his book *Let it Go!* Tony Evans says this about the cause of emotional strongholds:

> "But the kind of bondage the Bible calls a stronghold is rooted in either our own sin, in the sin of someone else, or in the fact that we live in a sin-tainted environment. You may have been abused as a child, and as a result of the abuser's sin against you, you are in emotional bondage as an adult.

> "Now you may be dealing with this in sinful ways with drugs or alcohol, or by taking out your anger on someone else. But in any case, the root cause of emotional strongholds is sin—which is why any solution that doesn't address the spiritual issue is not really a solution."

I had some violating experiences growing up that left an emotional residue running rampant in my life. I knew I needed to place these in isolation, but I had to acquire the skills to do it. The skill I needed was to acknowledge and accept what happened to me. I had to go through this process, but to be honest it felt as if I were fending for myself in shark-infested waters. I really missed my nest now. I felt cold and too weary to go on.

No experience in my life has left me more wounded, more vulnerable to the enemy's tactics, and more tempted to build idols than of the experience of being violated. In time, some of the wounds scarred over; others were infected and festering.

To be violated is to be breached without personal regard. To be breached means to be *ripped, torn,* or *ruptured.* For me it meant being exploited unmercifully at a vulnerable place and time. I allowed the power of the trauma to shock me into a silent stupor. It hurt, it was humiliating, and it was painful!

It was so powerful, in fact, that years after the actual occurrences the after-effects kept me from moving forward in many facets of my life. Even if I was able to move forward functionally, I wasn't able to do so emotionally until I learned and applied the skill of facing *it* and dealing with *it*.

Everything that surrounds those events—the sights, the sounds, the smells, the location, the time, the temperature—had left an indelible etch on my mind. Every time I heard *that* sound all the emotions connected with the event would come barreling up to the surface and debilitate me. Every time *that* fragrance wafted under my nose all that emotional intensity I thought I had quietly and successfully suppressed stirred up a gagging queasiness in my stomach. But oh how I tried to stuff it down, deep down, through mental acrobatics. This approach to dealing with my violation distorted both my *future* and my *present state* because it was fragmented and dishonest.

Just for the record, it took quite a while to acquire and use the skills to face and deal with the trauma. But applying the skill was the only way to confront and remove it from my heart because it was coiled around like long, strong vines knotted upon themselves and choking the major arteries of my heart. The long season of denial had allowed the vines to burrow down deep and gain a stronghold. Of course the vines also had a lot of leaves— also known as unresolved anger and unforgiveness.

Years after the violations, I was still trying to appear as though I were too strong to have sustained any injuries. I didn't want to admit that I had been "taken" or "played" because to do so made me feel violated all over again. This defensive pride aided my denial and kept me from being able to acknowledge the truth and deal with the anger and unforgiveness I harbored against the offenders. It kept me bound.

The fast track to distorted living is trying to exist and invest emotionally in both the past and the present. To live the abundant life means exerting all of today's energy on *today*. My growth was retarded because I had deformed myself by trying to dwell in two different realms—the past and the present. It was neither healthy nor realistic and it was all part of the enemy's design to steal my present and my future because I would not put my past where it belonged: behind. I could not live out my life wholly because I was fragmented.

I learned that if I ever wanted to petition heaven to get it back I would have to acknowledge and accept all that the violation stole from me. That foe did in fact win *that particular event*, but that was just one battle. The war being waged was for my entire life and the stakes were high: Would I remain "stuck" and live beneath my full potential or would I mount on wings and fly?

In my ministry, I have seen people live distorted lives due to their determination to beat a foe who had already come and gone. They resort to homosexuality or even prostitution ("I liked it," they say, deceiving themselves) or they become gangsters or womanizers ("I have always been the strong one," they say, deceiving themselves) or they become workaholics ("My employers need me and this corporation will live or die on my martyrdom," they say, deceiving themselves). Sexual violation, physical abuse, maiming criticism, or being unjustly fired from a job will keep such people living in the past if they refuse to acknowledge and accept that their foe did violate them. That battle is over and their enemy won. They can't go back! They must accept the truth and acknowledge what was lost if they ever hope to petition heaven to get it back.

It's like a teen who desperately wanted to go to a concert but could not afford to buy a ticket. The concert has come and gone, and yet that teen is still working overtime, wearing herself out, to earn enough money to purchase the ticket. It may be years later (or sadly never), after they have spent all of their life trying to earn the money, before they acknowledge or even realize the concert has long been over.

Although she finally earns enough money to buy the tickets, there are no tickets to be bought; the show is over. She missed it.

Denial works for a little while, but the true pain of the disappointment and the tricks the enemy uses to deceive her into wasting her life away on a futile effort seep out in myriad ways. And how tragic that so much of her life was lost living in past battles and never focusing long enough to win the war of her life and so she dies defeated, having been far less than she might have been.

It is painful for me to admit that I wasted years of my life and spent so much time, energy, and resources attempting to acquire what was no longer available. That is the tragedy. I needed to learn the skills so my foe could not rob my today and my tomorrow. Yesterday is gone. Chalk those battles up to a loss and focus on the entire war being waged for your life. You can win with God's help. He promised!

"I can do everything through him who gives me strength."
(Philippians 4:13 NIV)

Whether you accept it or not the enemy will constantly exploit the violation by using any and everything connected with the event—every emotion, odor, name, time of year, time of day, holiday—to beat you down in your mind with the goal of disabling and destroying you. He doesn't play fair. He cheats. It may be a flagrant foul, but he will commit it because it's all "fair game" to him.

Change the game by taking back all of the power the enemy leverages over you from those events by (1) acknowledging and accepting that they happened and (2) petitioning heaven to be restored. This will deal it a fatal blow and empower you to isolate it once and for all. No more emotional residue running rampant!

Your life and destiny depend on it.

Lesson #3—*Ratsah*

Trusting God with my physical needs, learning to deal with my foes, and gaining the ability to identify and isolate offenses were all giant steps along my pathway to healing. Applying these new skills helped me "de-clump" the needs of my longing heart. I was able to frame it more succinctly into three parts: (1) to know that God had pleasure in me, (2) to feel His Love, (3) to dwell daily in the confident security of God's Love for me.

Ratsah is a Hebrew word used about 54 times in the Old Testament of the Holy Bible. Fundamentally it means "to be pleased with" and is most often translated as "accepted," "delighted in," and "pleasure." *Ratsah* was most commonly used to express regard for an offering, as in:

> "And he shall put his hand upon the head of the burnt offering; and it shall be accepted for him to make atonement for him."
>
> *(Leviticus 1:4 NIV)*

Ratsah was used as God regarded an offering positively:

> "The Lord taketh pleasure in them that fear him, in those that hope in his mercy."
>
> *(Psalm 147:11 NIV)*

Ratsah was used as God regarded an offering negatively:

"He delighteth not in the strength of the horse: he taketh
not pleasure in the legs of a man."

(Psalm 147:10 NIV)

"Ye said also, Behold, what a weariness is it! and ye have
snuffed at it, saith the Lord of hosts; and ye brought
that which was torn, and the lame, and the sick; thus ye
brought an offering: should I accept this of your hand?
Saith the LORD."

(Malachi 1:13 NIV)

Humanity has a longing of the heart to feel the affirmation
of God, seeing as God has written His name on our hearts (Gene-
sis 3:22). His affirmation connects our spiritual reality to our
earthly experience. It keeps us from feeling fragmented and lost.
It makes us feel whole.

"I know also, my God, that thou triest the heart, and hast
pleasure in uprightness. As for me, in the uprightness of
mine heart I have willingly offered all these things."

(1 Chronicles 29:17a NIV)

It pleases God when we offer up our heart as a sacrifice. I
needed to consecrate my heart and set it apart as God's exclusive
habitation. I needed to strip away and circumcise all of the fleshly
desires from my heart and present it as a sacrifice unto the Lord.
What made my heart acceptable and pleasing to God was not my
being perfect, but my being *willing*—willing to bring my being
under the subjection of God's rule. As I grew and learned more
of Him and subjected my heart to His Spirit and Word, I began
to change, and my way was not so dark. To be found acceptable
and pleasurable to God truly is a miracle of God's grace!

Ratsah is extreme. Our need to get it from God is extreme,
and the cost God paid to make it available to me was extreme, for
it is only by the grace of God through the sacrifice of His Son and

through His righteousness and not my own that I have God's *ratsah*.

I believe that all human beings seek *ratsah* from God, whether their pursuit is conscious or subconscious. I see it as the *it* that people spend themselves to find. They go to bars and night-clubs, risk lying, cheating, and stealing in their own efforts to get the need for *ratsah* satisfied through people. They sacrifice themselves to almost any object to secure *it*. Weekend after weekend, day after day, they fail. All of these efforts fall short. To be found pleasurable to anything other than God does provide a measure of satisfaction, but nowhere near the depth of *ratsah* the heart longs for.

The attempt to get this deep longing satisfied by any source other than God results in emotionally masochistic self-abuse. I speak from experience. I went too far too often in my attempts to get this need met by mortal men. Oh the costly sacrifices I offered up to them.

Lesson #4—To Dwell in its Security

As I mentioned in the Introduction to this book, I knew God as the Great Almighty Judge and thus I feared Him. The story of Uzzah gives an example of why. To be honest, the story of Uzzah got under my skin to such a degree that I knew I had a major problem lurking about somewhere in my heart. And I did. I was a "pleaser."

After David achieved victory over the Philistines, he brought together chosen men to usher in the ark of the convenant as all the house of Israel rejoiced over its return and placement in Jerusalem, the City of David. When during the "ticker tape parade" celebration….

*"When they came to the threshing floor of Nacon, Uzzah
reached out and took hold of the ark of God, because
the oxen stumbled. The LORD's anger burned against
Uzzah because of his irreverent act; therefore God
struck him down and he died there beside the ark of
God."*

(2 Samuel 6:6-7 NIV)

Uzzah was struck down because He disobeyed. The New International Version (NIV) of the Holy Bible describes his act as "irreverent." God meant what He said when He gave the command that only the Levitical priests could touch the ark. I thought God should have graded on the curve with this one because I couldn't see any capital harm brought about by this apparently mild act of disobedience. Perhaps, I thought, God would have preferred to show a demonstration of His power as He performed a miracle to steady the ark. All in all, God really is capable of handling His own business and He does not make mistakes. Also, He is holy and is not to be trivialized—*no matter how apparently "small" the indiscretion.*

My drive to be accepted by people was such that if I were Uzzah, I would not have even been near enough to the ark to reach out and steady it. I would have dived in from the back of the celebrating crowd somewhere and no doubt waylaid a large number in the priests' processional to steady it.

Why?

Because I supposed, wrongly, that the favor of God and knowing Him intimately rested on my ability to win it. I equated His favor with the approval and acceptance of other people. If they approved of and accepted me, no matter at what cost to me, the result was my chance to dwell in His divine favor. It was a lie because *ultimately people have no power to make me feel secure.* All power comes from God. The powerful security that His unconditional Love provides is not earned but given! People cannot give it and their venomous glares cannot take it away!

I would have to trust the commands of God and obey. I had to change my selective hearing when He would say, "Hands off, Janeen, I got this all handled and worked out." Of course, I cannot stop God, so I got moved out of His way when I interfered. This always hurt my feelings. I did not understand at the time why I felt as though God was throwing me overboard on a regular basis…but now I do. God was trying to keep me from the self-inflicted wounds that result from disobedience.

People-pleasing is like shooting at a moving target. It's crazy even to try. I imagine that if I did try to steady the ark it would have probably fallen over anyway because of my fumbling ways. The entourage of worshippers may have tried to kill me because all of the holy things that fell out all over the ground and got dirty. They would have probably even cursed my grave blaming me—not the oxen or the cart—for the whole incident. They would have probably put an epitaph on my tombstone that read: *Here lies butter fingers, the blasphemer.*

I didn't want to be afraid of God anymore. And as I acquired the skill to redirect my focus from people to God, I was no longer driven by or focused on what people thought of me. The only thing that matters is what God thinks of me, and everything else flows out from that.

Lesson #5—Wall

I remember going to track meets in school to watch my sister run.

My favorite event was the 440, one circuit around the entire track. The best part was the "roll out" of the last curve! That always told the tale and distinguished the *stars* from the *scars*. Some would finish gloriously while others would fall from glory as they "hit the wall."

This term "hit the wall" is used to describe soldiers in training who were struggling as they neared the end of the grueling obstacle course. The last obstacle to be accomplished was to get over a 12-foot-high wall.

Some soldiers would be so exhausted and spent that the rope used to rappel them up and over the wall ended up hanging them instead. Too tired to jump as high as they could to reduce the amount of climb they had to do and allowing the rope to assist them, they ran head on and "hit the wall."

Smack!

From buoyant to belly up in the blink of an eye.

It would take minutes if not hours for their fatigued bodies to make it over that wall.

It is kind of funny to watch a track star that has "hit the wall." When the lactic acid kicks up and the oxygen gets sucked out they slow out of that curve immediately as if a bear has suddenly jumped on their back. They pump their heads and lose all form (let alone technique) attempting to throw their bodies toward the finish line wiggling, shaking, quaking, stumbling, just struggling along in a graceless fashion.

They have "hit the wall."

I could see how my efforts to seek God's *ratsah* from people-pleasing caused me to "hit the wall" apart from God as I gracelessly made foolish choice after foolish choice to secure it. I had been looking for protection, so I lived in harm's way. I had been looking for self-worth, so I tried to raise it by humiliating myself. I had been looking for someone to wipe my tears away until I finally picked up my hankie off the floor and did the honors as God granted me the right! I changed. No more wiggling, scooting, and working to get over that wall. No more wearing masks, people-pleasing, and idolizing my needs. I was going to ask God for the help I needed, just as I had asked him to help me learn to swim and navigate through the crashing waves.

To feel His Love I would have to trust Him more by opening myself to receive His touch. I had gotten the hang of my new swimming skills and had even gotten used to the fact that I may have to navigate the crashing waves for an unspecified amount of time…when suddenly I began to sink. Though I was cold and tired I had the will to swim on, but against my will I continued to sink. An external weight was dunking me down, not by grabbing my leg and pulling me down but by pushing me down from somewhere up near the top of my head…pushing me down into the deep dark water.

What now? My journey's next pathway.

CHAPTER 4

Love Unveiled

Oh no! The Seaweed's Got Me

I WAS ENCOURAGED and amazed as I tracked my progress. I had released myself and other people from the unrealistic expectation that they had to meet all the needs of my longing heart. I had learned and applied new skills that allowed me to frame my needs succinctly and "de-clump" them. These giant steps unveiled the next layer of the cause for my darkness. And though I was moving forward along the pathways, intimacy with God was still resoundingly missing.

> *"The engulfing waters threatened me,*
>   *the deep surrounded me;*
>   *seaweed was wrapped around my head."*
>
> *(Jonah 2:5 NIV)*

What I thought was seaweed choking me was actually a millstone around my neck. It was choking me because it was trying to slip over my head. The powerful pressure of the water's buoyancy was forcing it off of me, though I was still sinking under its great and oppressive weight.

I had gotten so used to bearing this burden on land that I had just accepted it as my "lot" in life. I had endured the strain on earth without objection. This weight, although lighter due to the lift from the seawater, was the reason for my speedy descent into the "bowels of the earth."

I was headed toward a more intimate relationship with God in which I would be dependent *solely on Him* to meet my needs.

It really cost me nothing to open my hand and release my grasp of the nest—my part was simply to let go and jump. It only felt costly during moments I doubted that He would rescue me if I were in *real* trouble... say drowning! This entire occasion turned out to be a great gain even though it did not always feel like it, especially now that I was descending at an uncomfortably quick rate. I would need oxygen soon and I needed to get this thing off my neck!

> *"Therefore, whoever humbles himself like this child is the greatest in the kingdom of heaven. And whoever welcomes a little child like this in my name welcomes me. But if anyone causes one of these little ones who believe in me to sin, it would be better for him to have a large millstone hung around his neck and to be drowned in the depths of the sea."*
>
> (Matthew 18:4-6 NIV)

I humbly asked the Lord to give me childlike faith to trust Him beyond my ability to do so. I didn't want to focus on my oxygen supply; I wanted to focus on this new pathway and where it would lead me. This leg of the journey had a big boot on the foot as it led me to the reality of sin in my life that I had to confess and repent (turn away from). In truth, I initiated some of these sins on my own; others were my response to the sins others committed against me. Sin was the composite nature of the millstone.

In his book *Let it Go*, Tony Evans says:

> "Emotional strongholds are fortresses the Enemy has built in our minds and hearts. They are built on his lies about who we are and what has happened to us or what we have done. This means that the root cause of these

problems has a lot to do with the Enemy's specialty, which is either trying to lead us into sin, or ensnaring us in our own sin or someone else's sin until we are completely bound up."

Ingredient number one: **Loss.**

Ice Cream Trip with Dad

It was a Sunday morning and I imagined that Dad and I would take a walk to the corner store to get an ice cream cone after church. "Mama," I said, "can you please do my hair real pretty?"

"C'mon, baby," she said. "I picked out this pretty pink bow to go in your hair that will match those pretty ruffles on your dress."

I was so excited I could hardly sit still for mama to finish gussying me up.

I was busy trying to think of what flavor ice cream to order because the corner store had so many to choose from. I was also thinking that it wasn't so much the really crunchy and sweet cones that made the trip so special. It was walking down the street, hand in hand, with my dad. Just him and me.

His hands were so big and strong. He was so tall.

Sometimes as we walked, we would play a game where he would rescue me from the "evil" cracks in the sidewalk. He would swing me over the cracks in the sidewalk to safety, after I would jump toward his protective arms.

Sometimes he would carry me on his shoulders part of the way. I would then pretend the ruffle on my dress was a fashionable hair wig I designed just for him.

Another special part was all the attention we got from the children in my community because most of them didn't have their dads around. A few didn't even know who their fathers were. As we strolled down the street, our neighbors and especially the bullies would know they couldn't taunt me because my daddy was with me.

I would be thinking, "Honey, just glare if you dare. I am pretty and I am with my daddy!"

I got even more excited as I thought how we would finally arrive at the counter. My daddy would say, "Baby girl, you can have whatever you want. Just pick!"

Dad would place our orders and hand over the money. The store clerk would love to see us coming because my dad always gave him a little tip for all the extra attention he gave us.

I would get three scoops, even though I knew I wouldn't be able to finish it all. I would put the "left over" in the freezer at home and eat from it through the week. It served as a gentle reminder of MY special time with MY daddy.

Such wonderful thoughts. I was getting down right fidgety now. My mama fussed at me to hold still so she could finish my hair as I struggled to contain myself as I thought of how my trip with Dad would end.

Out the door we would stroll, hand in hand, licking our ice cream cones. I imagined dropping my ice cream when we were just a few houses away from home, and I was devastated! Not only did it get on my dress but also now I would not have my reminder snack throughout the coming week.

What would I have to remind me of our wonderful time? What would I use to mark time toward his return next week? What would I have to show off to the children in the community?

I just knew we weren't going to turn around and go back, having traveled far from the corner store. But to my surprise, my dad didn't scold me. He took his napkin and wiped the ice cream off my dress and the tears from my face and told me not to cry.

"Ah, baby girl. No problem. Are you okay? We'll just go back to the store and get another one." His kindness and patience made me feel Love.

The emotion this story elicits exposes what this *imaginative* little girl longed for from her father. I was that daughter. My longing and wanting heart that yearned for this relationship produced an ingredient of that composite millstone that hung around my neck. The years I spent with this great emotional void sized my neck so that the millstone could fit it perfectly.

My heart stretched so far for so long to believe my dad would initiate and faithfully commit to maintaining a deep meaningful relationship with me—marked by his generous, unselfish, consistent overtures of patience and kindness in which I would be sheltered by his provision but mostly anchored by his love—that it eventually broke into myriad pieces.

This story tugs at my heart in ways far too painful to pen.

In real life, my dad left my mom, brother, sister, and me when I was a schoolgirl. My parents divorced soon after their second separation.

In reality there was never such a "sunny" trip to the corner store and never such a warm, loving relationship. There were no such excursions or affectionate interludes to help shape emotional health and model good relationships in this cruel, cold, cynical world.

The reality was that every day in his absence I was left to wander alone, emotionally longing and unfulfilled. Underdeveloped. Deformed. Not only was I bereft of the measure of protection and security a dad's presence provides, I did not even know how to express the immense feeling of loss.

How does a child explain or understand such an adult thing?

I coped the best I could by donning a mask that seemed to provide some measure of insulation against the great pain: Indifference.

Indifference adequately masked my frightful confusion and pain behind a false face that said to all the world: "I can take it or leave it."

Could I ever abandon myself to hope again? Would I even know how? Where was I going to get my emotional needs met? Would I grow out of the need for my dad's words and his touch?

I didn't care how all of these emotions would wash out in the *future*, what I really needed to know was what to do with all this pain *now*!

Would my eyes forever roam for that affirmation and long for the affection of a man? Could another man quench this wanting left by my father? What's a girl to do? What's a married woman to do? How do I carry this weighty emotion without reaping negative effects in relationships—especially relationships with men?

I loved my daddy *so* much!

I missed him!

And *oh my* how I needed him!

Composite millstone ingredient number two: **Rejection**.

It's a Family Affair

I was a member of a family that suppressed any *would-be* displays of raw, intimate, deeply passionate emotion: "There there now: there's no need for all that *gushy* stuff". We were genuine and passionate about each other, but very proud in that way that does not express itself outwardly. On many occasions in my life, I needed the family pride to give way to celebration, to exuberance, to some outward expression of passion. But our "family" pride kept it in check; they simply couldn't lay down the pride and get really excited. I wanted to be gushy. I wanted to feel the healthy touch of Love.

We all kept an emotional lid on our feelings. It ran so deep in my veins that my prayer, praise, and worship life was parched—dry and lifeless—from its effects. I never quite seemed able to arrive at that deep place I longed for when I was fellowshipping with God…it always stopped short of the real experience I was longing for. The torrential flow of spiritual tides I needed to refresh my heart and reclaim my perspective of who I was to God always seemed to get dammed upstream, so that I remained spiritually dry and emotionally parched.

Here's an example of how this pride manifested itself after it came to light that a cousin had been molesting me. I recall a rather stately inquisition—just the facts…but no tears or hugs. So I surmised that I *should* deal with pain and frightful emotional confusion by donning a mask.

I perceived that my own mother had done it as I watched her valiantly caring for her three children alone, while trying to process her own pain, grief, and disappointment over the failed marriage. I believed she needed someone—perhaps a family member—to get down on their knees with her and help pick up the emotional pieces and get "gushy." I felt as though most (not all) around her were more concerned about keeping their own masks on. It was too risky, you see, because masks can fall off and crash to the floor as you empathetically bend down and get involved with helping another pick up her broken pieces.

Maybe she cried on their shoulders behind closed doors to spare her children from seeing it. Maybe she didn't cry at all.

I didn't know about those "grown up" things, but what I do know is that there were masks: Tough exterior shells.

I was often devastated from my misplaced hope that they would actually work—cover or shield me from feeling pain and emotional confusion. My strategy of wearing them to cover me was also the formula for a stress stroke because it facilitated the demonic activity of blindness, deafness, and muteness. You have to be able to see, hear, and speak the truth in order to feel Love!

I didn't know how to "unplug" from seeking coverage and venture out into the open, drop the masks and take my chances. That's how it was that I allowed so much pressure to be placed on me to keep up appearances in my very public marriage. I was practically doubled over under the weight of all those masks I was carrying! I lost nearly all ability to feel and express my feelings honestly—raw and pure. My emotional responses were aimed at convincing people I was whole rather than to mirror the transparent wisdom of God. I thought my role was to keep silent, thinking that was what meekness meant. Wrong again…

> *"A fool gives full vent to his anger,*
> *but a wise man keeps himself under control."*
> *(Proverbs 29:11 NIV)*

Notice it says "control" and not "silent." I did not recognize the difference and so my ignorance advanced my strategy of wearing masks.

I would get so tired of switching between denial and indifference. I would often resort to my "steady" mask of indifference. I believed that responding indifferently and *looking stately* were the same thing. I had become so accustomed to appearing indifferent that I internalized it and became it.

Another factor that hampered my ability to feel and express my feelings purely and openly was my steadfast determination to appear tough. I believed that "emotional" people gave away control to a moment in time. I thought that was weak and foolish.

Why give someone or something control of you? This was a major problem for me for reasons I would only identify much later.

I got to the point that I honestly didn't understand how people could cry watching a movie or reading a book. I didn't understand how my peers could cry over the loss of a boyfriend or girlfriend. I couldn't even relate to tears from the loss of a loved one.

Were they really serious?

Were they really weak?

I was emotionally underdeveloped and lagged years behind. The loss—nay, the void—of a relationship with my dad was the "biggie"—the one millstone ingredient that haunted me because it was the only one that I couldn't seem to keep hidden neatly behind my mask.

I especially resented it when I sensed predators were looking in my eyes. They could see my desperate need—to have the gap my loss created filled or at least soothed—oozing from underneath the masks. I knew I was "found out" when those predators looked at me, but I had no means to cover myself in their presence.

In my deformed condition, I felt a need to apologize for my oozing and dripping, so I often resorted to another mask…it is too painful even to write its name. I can describe what it looks like on me though. I am easygoing by nature, but when I do not submit my nature to God's authority it gets bent to its extreme…. That mask would seemingly fall out of the sky and stick to my face.

I resented the hand that reached out to me in genuine compassion and would often slap it away because I could not accept it as "free" or "real." Surely no one would ever give me what I need—freely and without strings attached. I could *never* believe such a thing. And so I was left, still…wanting! It was tormenting.

That passive mask (oops, I wrote its name) was never one that I consciously chose. It was one donned subconsciously. In a moment it would just be on my face! I was too weak to remove it right away. I hated that aspect of being *out of control*. It always took a lot of effort to pull that mask off.

My masking was dangerous because the activity was veiled. I *existed* in my own internal world but *functioned* in the external world around me. It was like I was leading a secret life. I knew how to function like someone engaged in reality, yet in truth I was absolutely detached. It was not so much that I was a fake as I was just plain old *lost*.

Here's an example. My mom was determined to help me get out of my internal world and exist wholly in one place. She was concerned about me because she saw how detached I was from relating purely to others.

She was determined to break down my heavily fortified wall. She wanted to know, "What was going on with my *feelings?*" She was reaching past herself to get me to go further. So one night she took me up to the parking lot at her work. It was an incredible and admirable attempt. But I didn't talk to *anybody* and it suited me just fine. She tried desperately to reach out to me that night and I just sat in the car unmoved by her river of tears and emotion. Maybe I did shed a tear and say a few things, but if I did it was only to end this confusing emotional torrent as quickly as I could.

This is not how "we" handled things! After years of staunchly suppressing and practically ridding myself of the need to be "gushy" to the point that I had reached a state of near total disconnection from my own true emotions, I wasn't about to just open up and expose myself in such a way so easily.

I was totally disconnected from my own true emotions.

Let me tell you, it is a frightening place to be.

It sized my neck for a snug fit.

As a child my favorite Bible story was the Hebrew boys in the fiery furnace. I thought they were tough and I aspired to be like them! I gasped in admiration at their response to mean old King Nebuchadnezzar.

> *"Who cares what you do to us old king. We won't be ruffled by you one tiny bit. We'd rather die than to become unglued and all worked up behind your bullying!"*
>
> *(Daniel 3:16-18)*

Forgive my childhood paraphrase, but my perception of their strength became my battle cry to the world war raging inside me. I was gonna be stubborn and tough too, just as I thought they were. Not because I trusted Christ's power to deliver from bullies, but because I thought the power was in *my ability* to perform the task.

All those years later as an adult living outside the nest (and with God having my undivided attention—blub, blub), I could see that I didn't know how to deal with my failing marriage. It was jeopardizing my only source for Love—or so I thought. I was untouchable and previously there had been no room for potential pain of this magnitude. This thinking was hurting me, and I needed God's help to get it out of me. God mercifully plucked out these things because they weren't just going to wash off and float away under the pressure of the sea!

I was fidgeting with severe anxiety and desperate insecurity. What would I do if my marriage failed? My loss and rejection caused me to believe my marriage was the only source for Love. My distress caused me to cry out to God because the only source of Love I had ever known was being removed (seemingly) against my will.

> *"When my life was ebbing away, I remembered you, LORD, and my prayer rose to you, to your holy temple."*
>
> *(Jonah 2:7 NIV)*

Millstone ingredient #3: **Disappointment.**

Throwing My Weight Around

Kindergarten was a great period in my life. What I enjoyed most was the increased independence, especially riding the bus with the *big kids* to school, carrying my very own aluminum lunch pail, and having an older sister, Joyce, with me. These were my first memorable first solid steps toward my first conscious confrontation with my stubborn nature.

I was on the a.m. half-day schedule and Joyce, who by the way was a fiery second grader, attended school all day. By the time I was waking up from my afternoon nap Joyce would be returning home from school.

I so looked forward to her homecoming because I wanted to hang around her and the other *big kids* on our block. I thought that was living life to the fullest!

The problem would arise for me when playtime was over. It would be time to return home but I wasn't finished playing yet! On more than one occasion Joyce would have to deal with my stubbornness. With a few missing teeth she would call out very loudly her spirited description of my stubborn display, "Janeen, you are so hardheaded!"

"Janeen, it is time to go home and eat dinner," she would demand authoritatively. The right to make authoritative demands of me was bestowed upon her at my birth. (Hey, there are just certain rights that come with being the oldest).

"No, I'm still playing!" I would respond sharply. "I don't want to come home with you right now!"

This reply always gave me an audience of "ooooh's" from the *big kids*.

They were not "oooohing" because I was a *big kid*, too, who could boss others around, order my own world, and command the attention of my peers. They were oooohing because they knew my mama! My mama "didn't play that" childish (back talk) display thing.

"Okay Janeen," Joyce would snap back at me, "but you're gonna be in big trouble."

My fair-weather peer group would "ooooh" very dramatically once again, mocking my display of power and independence.

Joyce would leave very frustrated only to return in fewer than five minutes with these fateful words: "Mama said, you better come home with me or she's coming over here to get you herself!"

I would be so angry—not at Joyce who was only trying to intimidate me to good works by her firm demand. She was just the messenger. What I was really mad at was my resentment at being given a choice that was really no choice at all. I wanted the best deal out of this situation. I wanted to come home when I was good and ready, and I wanted my mother to lovingly accept this arrangement.

Besides, I wasn't hungry anyway.

The harder Joyce pleaded and tugged on me to come home with her, the more I pleaded and tugged in the opposite direction. The struggle typically ended with me sitting down on the ground.

That's right, I would simply park my bottom on the ground.

Joyce was a cute little girl with a featherweight body frame. I was rather chunky and cute, with a brick-solid frame. Once I sat down, she could in no wise cast me out of my trench.

Joyce loved me, and she would cry when I refused to come with her. I wanted to think that she was upset because my little fanny would pay a dear price for my folly. On the contrary. You see, along with my mother's decree for me to come home was the promise that my sister would be in trouble if she returned home without me!

Now in my adulthood I was suffering from all the residual effects of childhood. No excuses, but they do help to explain how such major blows of disappointment made it tough to embrace the call of God Almighty.

"Moses reported this to the Israelites, but they did not listen to him because of their discouragement and cruel bondage."

(Exodus 6:9 NIV)

Just as I was disappointed that I couldn't stay outside and play, I was disappointed I couldn't stay in my nest. Just as I rebelliously perched my fanny on the ground, I was doing essentially the same thing in my nest. And just as my rump didn't fare well as result of my childhood rebellion, the same was becoming apparent in my adult rebellion.

I wanted to stay in my nest. I was so frightened of a different source for Love. I knew this was dysfunctional, but it was also comforting because it was familiar. I felt like I was being given the same selection of "pseudo-choices" my mother gave me when I was a child—*you can stay or you can come, but either way you are going to come.*

I had to leave the nest...but before I finally jumped deep down I resented the request. Hindsight and parenthood help me understand that my mother had good reason to request—even *demand*—my presence at the dinner table as well as to order my world. I had to trust that although I could not see all the reasons or understand, God was requesting I let go and abandon myself to trust Him not because He was power hungry and capricous but because it was for my own good.

But for a period of time I was willing to self-destruct just to feel sovereign over my choices. My ego felt good but my rump didn't fare so well.

God's orchestration of His loving intervention and demonstration of care makes room for man's participation but only to the extent that we surrender to His will. There is no room for people's getting glory or taking credit from God. He alone secures the victory. He alone hands it to whom He wills it. But know that God is not going to force His will upon us. He prefers an invitation. And such is life (by design) that it is nearly impossible for me to escape the need to invite Him in. My asking keeps me sensitive to His directing my life.

I am sure that all honest parents would agree that if it were left up to their children to choose to take medicine that tasted bad, they wouldn't take it—no matter how desperately they needed it. A parent who gave in to such foolishness would have a very sick child and be guilty of negligence!

Thank God, He loved me too much to leave me to myself.

My determination to see these marital conflicts through to a *happily ever after* ending was not for the sake of the marriage but to preserve my security of Love.

Why?

God blew on my own efforts to keep me from myself (Psalm 119:71). Had I gotten my own way and been allowed to believe that I could secure my own security, I would never have come to know Him immediately. If I had been able to gain the deep experience of knowing God's Love and care in my life without having a deep walk with Him, I would certainly have chosen to live my life without ever accepting *His* invitation to care for me—to grow and learn of Him. It would have been His Love on *my* terms, relying on my own imperfect knowledge of what I needed. I would have been left incomplete with my heart still wanting. Why would I need God if I could do everything for myself?

If God had allowed me to choose that I would surely have been destroyed, all alone responsible for securing provision for all of my own resources—emotional, physical, and spiritual—in waging the daily battle life brings (without God's help). That is too tall an order for any human to fill.

Ingredient # 4: **Ambition.**

Miss Entrepreneur

Well there I sat at the head of the board table enthusiastically calling to order the first corporate meeting of a *bona fide* non-profit organization I founded. I willed it into being and here was the fruit of my grunt work.

Rancid!

Let me back up a little.

Soon after I was married, my entrepreneurial desires were pulling at me in a way I had not experienced before. I wanted desperately to own and operate my own business—almost to the point of recklessness. The severe shortage of resources and support made my dream seem impossible.

My entrepreneurial drive began early. Besides the proverbial lemonade sales, club fundraisers, and soliciting neighbors door-to-door for cash to pay for cheerleading uniforms (for a block squad a neighbor and I created) I can remember my first really lucrative business in sixth grade.

Growing up in a Los Angeles County suburb afforded me quite an experience and exposure to many ethnic and socioeconomic groups. The lower-to-middle class elementary school I attended was predominantly African-American but had a noteworthy Hispanic and Caucasian presence.

As a sixth grader I, like most of my classmates, gravitated toward the fads of the day. During that time a particular name brand school supplies and stationery was all the rage. They had branded pens, pencils, paper, backpacks, and the typical accompanying novelties geared toward children—all at a steep price for parents!

The only place around that sold these goods was a shopping mall several miles and a few cities away. Most of my classmates' parents had not the time, means, or desire to travel such a distance to purchase these novelty items. And they comparison-shopped the competition for a better deal. It made better sense to purchase the less expensive competition sold locally. Nonetheless, only the *name brand* product was coveted in my elementary school.

I remember going to this particular mall on the weekend with my allowance money of $5.00 and purchasing a few grape, cherry, and sour apple scented pencils and erasers. I couldn't wait to get to school just so I could use my new *name brand* school supplies! Sure enough, the Monday I got to school with that stuff I was the center of attention. Within five minutes, all but six children in the class ran over to ask me if they could use one of my pencils or erasers.

I enjoyed all of the attention and lent out one or two. By the end of the day I had a waiting list of potential users. I did the only thing I could think to do: I ran home and waited for Mom to get home so I could ask her to advance me my allowance. *Cha-ching!* I had to get to that mall quick to increase my inventory and social standing.

I had a heart, so I even let one underprivileged and socially alienated girl take a pencil home on a promise that she would return it. And you know what she said the next day in school? "I lost your pencil, and I am *so* sorry." "That's okay," I said, "Just give me sixty cents to replace it."

She happily gave me the money the next day and I learned quickly about *collateral* lending to protect an investment. From that day on, anyone who wanted to use a pencil would have to give me a quarter, with my promise to return it upon his or her return of my pencil or eraser.

As some of the children would take the pencils home, I began toting quarters to the mall, operating the principle of reinvestment. At collection time I got back a lot of pencils that were ugly, eraser-less, and faint in scent. So I sold those pencils for 50 cents and told my new customers that if they wanted to use the pencils they would now have to buy it at 60 cents.

Mind you, the pencils cost about 15 cents. But with so many selling points business was good! The use of these pencils brought even the most reclusive child an immediate elevation on the social scale. Many were more than willing to pay the price for such fame on the playground. That was priceless—even if it meant going without lunch.

During quiet time in class after the long lunch period, I would daydream about hearing the pencil sharpeners whizzing all over the school as a result of all the new pencils I would distribute. Word of mouth proved once again to be the strongest form of advertisement, as children from other classes placed orders for pencils and erasers.

Well not even three weeks later my business was good and growing at a pretty fast rate. It was a *bona fide* success, and I sat there basking in business glory with wadded-up dollar bills and loose change all over my desk. As I slowly leaned back in my chair enjoying my success, my peers were resting with their heads on their desks. It was quiet time after the long lunch recess period. My daydream of palm fronds blowing in the gentle breeze and sunny seashores adjoining my millionaire estate was disturbed by my concerned teacher standing over my desk. She was blocking my sunlit tropical vision. She was also one of our neighbors from who I had solicited for money for the cheerleading team my neighbor and I devised.

As she gently leaned over my desk and began gathering up my profits and working capital, she expressed her concern and whispered caution: "You need to put this away because it won't be the pencils and erasers they will come after you for."

I had never considered the threat of my personal safety from the playground bully. I had more than lunch money at this point and I would be a prime target for her! The reality was that now that my older sister was attending junior high school at another campus my back felt a little too drafty for me to confidently continue in this very lucrative business.

As the school day ended, my teacher gave me back my profits and working capital, which she had safely stored in a safe (her desk drawer), and I settled up with all of my customers and ended my venture.

I started off having fun as I watched the money roll in and ended up with something profound. I stumbled upon what I wanted to be when I grew up: a businesswoman.

I tried to deny it. I tried to pretend I was floating through life when really I had a millstone around my neck that weighed me down as well as an even bigger, heavier mask to cover the big thing up. The mask was so huge in fact that for a while that I had even forgotten the truths that lay underneath it.

These millstone ingredients and so many more were like seeds that had been systematically planted in my life that over time grew and impeded me with their long, strong vines. Those seeds and saplings grew and I tried to abandon the negative fruit they bore in my life by covering them up.

I promised myself that I would see to it that I was unscathed by every negative seed planted in my life. I would not have any weeds in my life that needed pulling because nothing was going to affect me unless I allowed it to….

Yeah, right!

I looked like a mad woman as I denied the obvious existence of the mammoth-size trees and vines growing in my life. They were now towering and shading over me and blocking my easy access to the warmth and light of Sonshine. But had you asked me about them, I would not even have acknowledged them. You could have even placed my hand right on them and asked about them and still I would have craned my neck and said, "What greenery are you talking about?"

In some cases my temperament created a fertile environment for the seeds to grow in, but to be honest in most cases the real nutrient that enriched the soil was my fear and pain! It was all really so tormenting. I felt abandoned by my Heavenly Father because I thought He should have rescued me without my having to ask. You see, asking would have required me to face my self-deception first. *Ownership.*

I was beginning to feel as though my existence was insignificant and meaningless. The pain and denial in all this vining foliage made them root deeply and knot securely in my life, against my conscious will.

Movement On The Wheel

So back to the board meeting…I had founded a non-profit organization, executed my own utility patent for a product I invented and hoped to sell, started a helium balloon delivery service network, and even opened a restaurant (just to name a few)—all to help our downwardly spiraling economics.

I asked: "God, I have the potential here to make some much needed finances for my family, why are You holding it all up! You own the cattle on a thousand hills, will You just give me one? "

Each enterprise failed. And with each failure, I felt even more abandoned by my Heavenly Father. He blew each of my endeavors to shreds.

Why? How could my entrepreneurial efforts have been a sin?

Surely, they must have been "sin" for God to blow them to smithereens, I thought. The truth was that while each business endeavor had a good and wholesome idea, I was motivated more by my resentment and desire for financial freedom than for any higher purpose. I believed that financial freedom would rid my need for Love. My flesh would become strong and satisfied to the point of smothering my yearning heart.

I was trudging in a chaotic sphere of confusion and disorder. It was so miserable! I was really stuck. I simply could not get my mind around how God could will failure for me when my efforts were directed toward getting more of Him! So my first approach to appease my questioning heart was to resign myself to my own reasoning.

Perhaps I was just too unworthy to have a successful enterprise. I had even begun to allow these failures to keep me from considering that God really had placed those hopes and dreams in my heart and that He would bring them to pass one day, in spite of me! I had been gifted with administrative skills, a keen business acumen, creativity, and ingenuity. But though these gifts are strong and easy to access, my *heart* was hard.

Back then I thought I was God's overlooked, finished masterpiece, but I realize now that I was indeed a real *piece of work*. So with a gentle swing of His hammer, God allowed my marital conflict and business failures to break me, unveiling my real fragmented heart's pain: God's working of my human clay.

God was molding my heart to the image of Christ.

The Potter was a Master at His craft, but I kept jumping my human clay off His potter's wheel (His will) and squishing down onto the cold hard floor. His process of molding my heart was hard, tedious, and slow.

If I couldn't very well deny that I needed the work, at the very least I wanted Him to be finished...*soon!* Actually, what I really wanted was to avoid this process altogether. Every time I pointed to a failed business or to my failing marriage as a cause of my pain, I jumped off the Potter's wheel.

While I can confess that business and marital failures blocked the easy clear view of the Sonshine they also inadvertently helped me maintain some measure of pliability before the

Potter. My jumping, however, did cause a delay in the Potter's work on me.

Thank God He is stronger and wiser than I am!

Spiritually, emotionally, and physically I was so dry, but my selfish ambition kept me trudging through the Christ-less desert. The enemy was also at work during this time wreaking his typical cruelty. He constantly held the mirage of security and liberty through a human relationship or economic stability before me. I wanted emotional security and liberty, yet all I ended up with was a mouth full of sand!

I was deceived into believing that I was struggling with business or marriage, but all along I was struggling with God! I was deceived into believing that God was against me with each failed endeavor, but He was for me! I was deceived into believing that God despised my ambition and desire for liberty, but those can only be truly found in Him!

But there was pain in the molding: It still hurt every time I resisted His gentle hands.

God knew my heart and thoughts. He knew I was faking! A failing marriage and business were not my issues. Embracing His Love was. He knew my heart's desire for financial freedom was not to "help out" the family. My intention was to afford myself fare to Tarshish!

Come storm at sea and a great shipwreck, my heart was not going to turn back once I earned my ticket to sail. No, it wouldn't have done well for me to get rich and set out on a luxury liner for Tarshish. For then I would have justified my departure in a way that worldly society would celebrate. Everything around me would have enabled an easy transition to a new life for me without … *him.*

The danger of this ease was that it would keep my focus on the natural reasons for making my departure and leaving little to no room for examining my heart's condition—what He was working behind the scenes in my spirit, the supernatural reasons. It would have been too deeply rooted in the practical reasoning of men.

I desired the financial freedom not only because it would provide me with a way to leave my husband, but each of those ventures were also poised to take the seat on the throne of my heart. Time and time again I had created a vehicle through my gifts and talents to get my starving needs for significance, value, and self-worth met. I knew that my needs were too profound for any human to meet. God loved me too much to allow me to look to something temporal for a deeply spiritual, eternal need.

Now began a profound spiritual awakening. The unseen realm really had now become more real to me than the seen realm, just as the Bible speaks of (2 Corinthians 4:18). The revelation of the great deception of presuming that my righteous-looking behavior could hide the intentions of my wayward heart opened up the floodgate to other areas of deception that bound me—such as: I realized I had been trying to use my administrative gifting to manage demonic activities that were sent to destroy my home. My first husband dabbled in a few activities that opened the door wide for lasciviousness to come in.

Its mark was evident all over my home and finances. Its destruction wrought chaos and confusion that brought a steady onslaught of stress as I foolishly tried to utilize my gifts of administration to "manage" it.

It wore me down and wore me out! You can't manage demons! You have to cast them out!

How? Truth!

It is the only way. The only weapon in spiritual warfare.

I was tempted to believe that my gifts and talents in the area of administration could handle the chaotic, confusing, and out-of-control personality of the demon. My wayward, prideful heart enabled it to pounce destructively and uncontested in my home and assist in its evil, destructive plan for my family by not calling on the Truth!

My daily life was like raking leaves in a tornado. It kept me too busy, distracted from what was important, frustrated, and more determined to get all the leaves inside the trash can! I can see how my efforts to earn a loving close union with God and receive His care as well as blame shifting made me move off His will and splat onto the cold hard floor.

My pain, emotional unavailability and stonewall stubbornness, rebelliousness, and ambition were all ingredients in my millstone.

That weight about my neck made me hit the floor even harder. If I would have just sat still long enough to allow the Potter to remove this intrusive object then my mistakes would not have been as painful. But all the masks and efforts to cover the real me delayed my processing. It hurt!

As more of my *ish-you's* and the results of my grunt work were crushed out of me from the pressure of the deep kneading of my spirit, I began struggling for air. At this point so much debris was now swirling around me, including the entire exploded millstone with all its tiny bits whirling around, that visibility was near zero. I stopped squinting and swatting the particles in an effort to see, and I closed my eyes in trust of God's promise to care for me.

"Come to me, all you who are weary and burdened, and I will give you rest. Take my yoke upon you and learn

*from me, for I am gentle and humble in heart, and you
will find rest for your souls. For my yoke is easy and my
burden light."*

(Matthew 11:28-30 NIV)

God was still seated on the throne of heaven and I knew He
was watching over me, so I released the last little piece of twig
from my nest that I had been secretly holding on to since my
jump.

"Lord, let your will be worked out in my life—*whatever* the
cost may be. Amen."

Well my giant ocean liner pulled up. While the smell made
for no vacation cruise on the inside, at least it did have air that I
could breathe.

CHAPTER 5

Wrestling Love Down

BEARING THAT MILLSTONE enabled certain predispositions that created a hazy dysfunctional filter through which I saw God. Ultimately, what was in my way was "my way." That's the brutally honest characterization of the hazy dysfunctional filter. It obstructed my ability to apprehend True Love. *My Way* was in my way. I needed help to aid me in wrestling it down off of me.

This next pathway would bring the most tedious and critical steps because I had to consciously engage my will as I never had at any time in my life. I had to dethrone every approach to getting my needs met that were born apart from an intimate relationship with God. I truly served "my way" as an idol.

> *"But the LORD provided a great fish to swallow Jonah, and Jonah was inside the fish three days and three nights. From inside the fish Jonah prayed to the LORD his God. He said: 'in my distress I called to the LORD, and he answered me. From the depths of the grave I called for help, and you listened to my cry.'"*
>
> *(Jonah 1:17, 2:1-2 NIV)*

Sanctification

The trip over the side of the boat was free of charge! But this isolation cost me my emotional spare time as it exposed me to a depth of loneliness that haunted me. I now understood what I had heard others say they experienced—being in a crowded room *yet all alone.*

When my first husband and I were legally separated I returned to work at a bank but was on public assistance. It was miserable and humiliating! There was always just enough as the children and I lived from week to week, paycheck to paycheck, cupboard to cupboard. I struggled with the children alone. These would prove to be the loneliest and hardest days of my life.

When God separated me from the familiar world of my nest, my heart underwent a transformation before my very eyes. My physical body continued to have its natural experience in the world, but my heart was having an experience in the spiritual world. Not that I became a split personality, but the individual components that make me—body, soul and spirit—were more pronounced during this time.

The isolation and tough time helped me discover and focus on each component. This was the prelude to my sanctification process.

So, what does that word *sanctification* mean? I thought sanctification meant to be "old and mean in the name of Jesus." As a child, I can remember a "group" of elderly people in my church who referred to themselves as being "sanctified." They seemed to take great pride in that distinction, to the point of shaming and even shooing the "little lesser ones" from their presence because they had not "arrived yet" to their level of Christian achievement and righteousness.

They were "clean" and all others were "dirty." They sat up "front" and we were to keep in the "back." I decided that I *never* wanted to have the title of "sanctified" because I didn't want to ever be old and sour (not to mention *sorely unfashionable*). It also seemed too hard to ever attain. Besides, I wanted to be expressive and what they called sanctification looked like bondage!

I understand now that sanctification means to be set apart by God, for God.

"I am my beloved's, and my beloved is mine."

(Song of Solomon 6:3a KJV)

As I sat like Jonah in the belly of this great fish, I noticed that the isolation allowed me to apply what I had learned so far on my journey to each component of me—body, soul and spirit. I also noticed that my labored breathing was due not just to my disgust of the odors, the wrestling match with the millstone, or the exhausting trip down into the deep. It was the balance of my *ish-you's* surfacing, hindering my progress on this journey. I didn't have a pressurized cabin in my submarine fish, so the crushing pressure in the deep began to press them out of me.

The discharges pressed out of my spirit were surprising because of the material they were made of—dark looking, globby stuff, yet familiar in their form. I had to body slam them after they came out of me because they were still alive and attempting to climb back inside of me for their protection from the crushing pressure of the deep sea. My rudimentary prayer was the pressure that was pressing them out as I had time on my hands and no human interaction to distract me from this task.

I wanted to be free of them but some were so embedded that they needed to be plucked out. I couldn't pluck them out on my own so I asked God to help me. Besides, I had created such habits of clinging to them that I simply did not know how to expel them.

God prepped me for surgery and grabbed the scalpel. All I had to do was lie there and watch the movie screen He provided to focus me. The name of the show playing was "Hindsight 20:20."

He started cutting and I started crying. Not in pain, but in cleansing and healing. I had no need to fear death. He loved me and promised to give me all the strength I needed to recover and continue along this pathway after He was finished with the spiritual surgery. The cleansing was a result of "them" being removed from me, and healing was a result of me finally *asking* God to help and heal me in the deepest way. And just as He promised, He did.

> *"What causes fights and quarrels among you? Don't they come from your desires that battle within you? You want something but don't get it. You kill and covet, but you cannot have what you want. You quarrel and fight. You do not have, because you do not ask God. When you ask, you do not receive, because you ask with wrong motives, that you may spend what you get on your pleasures."*
>
> *(James 1:1-3 NIV)*

I was going to have to let Him rid me of "my way" once and for all and release me from the bondage my pride caused by trying to obtain True Love, "My Way."

The Shoe Story

I was so young during my first marriage, and we were both trying to figure this whole marriage thing out and define which roles and responsibilities were whose.

I hardly had any devotional time with God anymore. I heard sermons and talked to God about the things I wanted to do, but I do not recall ever examining the contents of my heart before him in a deep intimate way. As a result, I placed my first husband on the throne of my life with crown and scepter. The outfit looked good on him during the "honeymoon" period, but it faded quickly and lost its luster as the wedding officially ended and the marriage began—which came during the first few weeks of our second anniversary. Something about having a *lord* over me made me feel safe and secure.

He enjoyed it that first year. He was the king and getting the hang of wielding his scepter. As the queen I was still adjusting my tiara. We both thought that was how things were "supposed to be." It was cute, I thought.

"Janeen, honey, get off the phone...Let's go here or there or let's participate or not," he would command. He totally dominated and I thought it was wonderfully wild.

I remember vividly the day I offered *him* the throne to my life.

He was in the U.S. Navy and came home one day from the ship he was serving and told me that we were going, *right now*, to buy me a pair of shoes. My shoes had a hole in the bottom.

I felt ashamed really at my need and tried to convince him that I would be all right and that we should just save the money instead of spend it on "little old me." He was confused at my response to his command because this image of a "soft," indecisive, and extremely passive Janeen is not what he knew me to be. That mask just fell out of the sky it seemed and stuck to my face without my request.

Oh, Dad....

Nonetheless, at that moment, strong, independent, and progressive immediately became who *I WAS*.

I reasoned that we shouldn't go but he wouldn't take no for an answer and further told me to get ready because we were going to the shoe store *NOW*.

I remember being disagreeable with him in the store and trying to put on airs as if there was nothing in the store that would suit my taste or style. The truth was that I hadn't been in a shoe store that sold "good" shoes in so long that it was just an emotionally weird feeling. I had worked in clothing stores in high school and college and had not been in the position of having to depend on someone to completely meet my physical needs in a few years.

I was also accustomed to the sunny southern California wardrobe—living year-round in cheap sandals and shorts. But all of that was in my past now. Winter was looming in my new New England home, and I had to adapt immediately. My need for shoes had to be addressed!

I wrestled with my mask, but I was losing and coming unglued. I had to come face-to-face with the reality that I would have to completely depend on *him* for my physical needs during the next few months, until we relocated and transitioned out of and away from his military service.

I was so confused about what I was feeling as I stood in that shoe store looking at shoes. I was angry, ashamed, and in denial that I was shaking in my boots at my new position of dependence on *him*. I had looked for work, to no avail, which left me feeling and believing that I was useless and helpless. We didn't have a car, and their public transportation didn't compare to what I was used to in southern California (if it could be compared at all).

I was not equipped nor prepared to dig deep enough to analyze all this emotion gushing out of me in the shoe store but I was choked up—especially seeing my mask now in bits about my feet. I was traumatized! Did I feel secure about my decision to wed him now after all?

I accepted the shoes and he paid for them at the register. I hastily reached out for the bag. He took it from me and told me to throw the shoes I had on away, and from the look on the face of the cashier I knew I should have. But in grand style I "saved face" and donned a mask of my choosing.

In attempt to salvage control of my physical needs, I told him that it would be good just to keep the old shoes so as not to wear out the new ones. He was reluctant, but he accepted that and insisted that while we were out in public, *I was not* wearing those holey shoes.

"Janeen, put those old shoes in the bag and put on the new ones *now,* please!"

So instead of handing them over to the cashier, I put those old shoes in the box and carried them out of the store in the bag.

I felt so ashamed on the way back home. How would I ever repay him for meeting my physical needs? How would I deal with being out of control of directly meeting my own needs?

I obeyed, followed, and trusted in my way to get my practical material needs met. *My way* was my idol I served. It kept me from praying.

Hurdles began to come up. In truth, the hurdles were welcome. In truth, I nearly demanded them because they made me feel worthy of the physical provision I credited him with providing for me. These hurdles were simple at first. He wouldn't pick up his clothes off the bedroom floor after changing or in the bathroom after a shower and I would do it. Then he would no longer scrape his plate let alone take it in to the kitchen nor offer to help with the dishes at all.

I took care of things and picked up the slack with no questions asked. No moan, no groan, no gripe. I would raise no objection nor confront him at all! Neither did the inconvenience it sometimes caused me *matter at all*. It did not even merit consideration. But instead of feeling deserving or worthy I began to feel worthless.

I jumped over each hurdle that came up, no matter how much strain it caused me, but the prize of value, honor, and respect was always just out of reach. I kept running and jumping for him, but with each step I abdicated the power of my life over to the hands of a man.

> *"I am in deep distress. Let me fall into the hands of the LORD, for his mercy is very great; but do not let me fall into the hands of men."*
>
> (1 Chronicles 21:13b NIV)

Granted, I had extremely low self-worth, which is why I entered into such a vicious track-and-field event in the first place. Why did I feel out of control? Because I took my eyes off the One who enabled *him* to provide for me as being the Ultimate Source. I crowned *him* king instead of *Him* as King! I could not see that I was going to be taken care of through God because that required me only to trust God *His way*.

My faulty and sinful perspective altered me. It created a filter through which every pursuit of getting my needs met centered on winning *him* over independent of The Provider. This included meeting whatever conditions or expectations *he* demanded of me. It bent my talent, gifting, and personality traits out of whack because they were no longer centered on the healthy growing love relationship with the Giver.

A Date with Nostalgia

Here's an incident that shows how deep in the valley I descended...I went to visit my mother at her home in California—alone—for a long overdue visit and vacation. I went to recurperate because I was mildly injured in a car accident in New England. (What is bizarre is how that opportunity was afforded me, but I will leave those details for another time).

The first couple of days, I slept.

It was wonderful and strange. The days and nights just kind of ran together. And it took me 48 hours just to adjust my thinking. It was hard to believe there was no one around trying to breach the quarters of my personal space.

When I finally emerged, rested, my mom suggested that I get in touch with some of my old friends. So I caught up with a few of them and set a date and "the girls" and I went out to dinner.

What should have been an evening full of giggles, grins, and photo ops turned out to be traumatic. I had been too isolated for too long in my little new *hometown*. I was sorely unprepared for interacting with "young progressing adults" in the big city.

For starters, I remember when my friend came to pick me up I did not even know what kind of car she was driving. At my question of the make and model of her car she thought I was just being "crazy old Janeen" from *back in the day*. But I really didn't know. I felt as though I had been in a coma. My years of living so isolated had proven to be a type of grave after all and not a healthy empowered choice for the way *I* wanted to live my life. I was existing and not really living.

To see "the girls" again and hear their stories of life after being *married with children* or even the stories of those who chose the *single life* in *Corporate America* unsettled me. Although I had maintained the same dress size I wore in high school (nearly 10 years after graduation) and many of them had not, they all appeared far better on the inside to me: *Strong*.

Then the moment I had dreaded shot me right between the eyes. I wanted to run away and duck down and hide when they asked me what my life was like. My response? I burst out into hysterical laughter near the point of tears. They then chimed in with laughter and joking. One said, "I thought when I was going to see you tonight, girl, you were gonna be wearing a habit."

They thought my laughter was borne of strength. They assumed the reason I still had my high school figure was that I had made a personal commitment to myself. They thought my non-responsiveness was coy, as though I were teasing them.

I hit the "dress size" mark! So on the outside it looked as though I was strong because that was *all* they could see. Unfortunately, as they continued, I realized that the outside was all they ever truly saw. My masking kept them from seeing me and disabled them from discerning my need now. I could see that God saw me.

But I know my laughter-to-tears was a result of their question's undoing me. I was weak. I was broken. They thought my figure was the gauge of my strength when it was really an indicator of my level of despairing weakness.

I had maintained the same dress size for over 10 years in part because I had "controlled" my eating. (More on this a little later…). I was so afraid of being found in need of an entire wardrobe and I wanted to avoid vulnerability to manipulation in this area. So I maintained control of my size at an almost reckless pursuit by "conditioning" myself.

I remember learning about "conditioning" in a psychology class. Consistent, sustained conditions can create behavior that is predictable, automatic, performed without thought: "Auto Pilot." Engaged thinking and processing does not occur until the conditions are changed.

The following is a brief example of this concept: If a stray kitten found a bowl of milk at 5:00 p.m. everyday at my back door, come rain or shine that kitten would be found there at my back door purring for milk at 5:00 p.m. The kitten may even starve to death if after days I did not set the milk out for it. Hopefully, this change of events of not putting milk out at 5:00 p.m. would cause the kitten to get out of the "auto pilot" mode and hunt.

Anyway, I began to apply this "conditioning" to myself to control my size. When I would get hungry and was feeling that my clothes were a little too snug, I would eat ice. The process of placing the ice in my mouth and biting, chewing, and swallowing caused my brain to communicate to the rest of my body that I had just ingested food.

For about 20-30 minutes my stomach wouldn't growl, and after that time expired I was always preoccupied with tending to the children, feeding or cleaning, that when my glucose level demanded "real" attention I was busy enough to suppress my dietary needs.

As with many women with low iron, to cope I ate ice. I was so miserable I would go through a 10-pound bag of ice every four days. When there was no bag of cubed ice in the house, I would take a hammer and crush the ice I'd made by filling water into a plastic sandwich bag. I knew I had a problem. My dentist told me that my teeth, albeit straight and white, had been eroded to the size of someone nearly triple my age. I cannot even begin to tell you of all the headaches and migraines I triggered due to the extreme chomping, shaking my brain so.

Pica is the name of this condition. It is defined as: an eating disorder; the compulsion to swallow non-food items. It is derived from the Latin word for the Magpie bird (picus) which is known for eating indiscriminately. *Pagophagia* is the type of pica I had. Some doctors say it is the *result* not the *cause* of iron deficiency while others say it is the cause. While the earlier form of my condition was directly related to iron it became a psychological condition. I needed help.

"The girls" wouldn't have believed the truth of the tale even if I had been daring enough to tell it all. They probably would have laughed me to tears in utter disbelief.

Unfortunately, they assumed that their question needed no verbal answer. So they did not press for one. My physical appearance was a sufficient response to their query—so they thought. But, oh, I really felt a need to share my life experiences with "the girls." I wanted to fume, cry, and scream! I wanted to "let it out"! I wanted to purge myself of the truth about how low my self-worth and esteem had plunged. I wanted to release it.

I wanted them to help me dig out of the emotional hole I had burrowed into. I wanted them to pray for me and surround me with love to help me acquire the courage to change. I wanted them to accept me where I was. But I refrained. I donned the stately mask that I knew they would like. That was sadly and painfully the only "Janeen" they had ever really known. I, again, covered up the dark truth underneath.

To feel the Love of God required that I disrobe in His presence, not theirs. Masking was "my way," and it served to keep me from getting "my way" with God for many years. Transparency in a relationship is necessary, but people have imperfect and limited knowledge. It would take more than a lifetime to explain all I had been through and the impact to my girlfriends. They could understand on a certain level, yes, but not like God.

I obeyed, followed, and trusted in my way to get my need for self-actualization met. My way was my idol that I served. It kept me from prayer—which was the very lifeline needed to successfully wrestle down "my way" and expel it!

Self-Centered Self-Worth

During that visit to my mom's house, I also got a chance to see a few of my sister's friends—the "big kid's friends." They came to visit me at my mom's house. It had been years since I'd seen them and it was refreshing.

By then my mother had moved from the house we all shared with my grandmother during our junior and senior high school years. Back then my grandmother's house was the "hang out" house. It was always teeming with "big kids" from the neighborhood! One of the neighbors from the old house kept in touch with my sister and got in touch with me at my mom's house. He wanted to see me.

The phone rang and my heart raced when I saw his name in the caller identification window flash on the little screen. I was so excited to hear from my old neighbor. It had been more than 10 years since I last saw him. The sound of his voice was like a hyperspeed time machine that flung me back to that skinny cheerleader I used to be in high school.

I had forgotten all about her and wasn't sure that I wanted to remember who she was. When I said "I do" in marriage I buried her; at least I tried to. I thought that that was necessary for being a good Christian wife. At any rate, this entire vacation so far was just what the doctor ordered. When he invited me to have dinner, I admit I was looking forward to traveling down more of those familiar memory lanes. I was looking forward to seeing him. That fresh recollection of that skinny cheerleader made me warm up to the idea of reacquainting myself with her, too.

Nostalgia, as I shall refer to him, had professed faith in Christ and married about two years before I did. I was confident that the time we would spend together would be relaxing and "safe." Oh, the stories and events he witnessed as *our* neighbor made for a lot to reminisce about.

Well, there we were dining on some great Mexican food (which I had been craving for years) and having a great time recalling the "good ol' days." You see the power of this friendship was just that—we were just friends. Never an intimate hug or kiss between us.

He and I spent time together largely because we were neighbors. He lived down the street from my grandmother. He was within a year or so of my sister's age and went to the same high school. He was like a big brother to me.

He could come over while I would have a male visitor over and his presence caused no friction at all because everyone knew the nature of our friendship. He did not have to be invited over, as all others who were calling on me did (*that was a must!*).

He could come over and talk to my sister, or he could come over and talk to my mother or my grandmother. His reason for paying a visit was rarely me. Everyone in the house had his or her own relationship with him, including our television.

When I didn't have an escort to a party or was just plain bored, we'd go out. We both enjoyed dancing. And dance we did till the curls were sweat out of my hair. Broken down cars or motorcycles were against my self-imposed social protocol, but his were so much fun to ride and push. Well, dinner was nearly over when like a lightning flash came the question I had tried to duck from "the girls."

"So, Janeen, tell me…are you happy?"

I couldn't compose my stammering tongue. So I just cooled down and kept my composure, smiled, donned my mask, and sat there as he offered his speculation.

As he began to measure how he thought my husband should be treating me against the standard I required of all my teen suitors those 10-plus years ago, I tasted something weird in my mouth.

Blood.

I was nibbling on the inside of my jaw so hard I was bleeding. So I readjusted my slipping mask, sipped my cola, and kept my cool. I affixed the mask tighter, just as I did every time I was confronted with a potential emotional monsoon. I finally mustered the courage to look up from my soda glass, now dry of every trace of condensation, as his "investigative reporter" style questioning ended. It was quiet for a moment or two, and I had committed to look up, on the count of three, unmoved and confident.

When I did, I found him staring at me.

Warnings flashed again!

His gaze was different; he knew it and I did, too.

Was it the blinding glare of the lights reflecting off the water drops I had been concentrating on clearing from the outside of my glass that fuzzed my vision? Was the image of the little girl left longing in my childhood there in those droplets, or did I see her needs being met in the reflection of his eyes? Could he wipe the tears away and redeem the time I had spent paying the price that my search for Love had cost me? We immediately called it a night and parted company. We didn't see each other again for a few years after that date—a reunion that would prove bittersweet.

I could not see myself as whole because I would not look through the eyes of Christ. I knew Nostalgia, the girls, my mother, and the others, and I could see myself through their eyes. But that view was imperfect. To feel the Love of God, I would have to spend time with Him and get to know Him so that I could see myself as whole through His eyes. But at the time I was obeying, following, and trusting in *my way* to get my emotional needs met. My way was an idol I served. Again, it kept me from praying!

And so I sought out relationships with other people to meet the needs of my heart, and this got me in some illegitimate unions. The enemy baited me with a mirage of emotional security and satisfaction. I saw the sharp point on the hook but in my foolish, desperate, selfish anger I bit the bait.

In his book *Getting Closer to God*, Erwin Lutzer says this:

"When God is silent and appears indifferent to our needs, a climate is created where idolatry flourishes. Where we turn when we are desperate speaks volumes about where we are in our walk with God. Whether we draw closer to God or turn away from Him depends on how well we know Him. When we feel that God has failed, an idol stands ready to deliver us. The closer we are to God the closer we want to get; the farther we are from Him the more attractive idols become."

Hungry people will go out of their way to look for food; starving people will hunt and kill for it. I allowed my starvation for relational intimacy to drive me to recklessness. Instead of placing my needs before God, I placed them in my own hands and poured it on people.

I failed to mind how my extra time was being spent—not just in terms of physical activity but in terms of emotional energy, too. "An idle mind is the devil's workshop," the elders at my childhood church would say. I did not fill up on God; rather, I entered into illegitimate unions to satisfy my desires for intimacy. This extended to gossip with family members and unhealthy sharing of secrets.

I needed to get off the phone, get out from in front of the television and fast and pray. You see, when my desire for God becomes greater than my desire for anything or anyone else, my heart will always become untangled and free from illegitimate unions.

Queen for a Day

I obeyed, followed, and trusted in my way to get my need for significance met, too. My way was the idol I served. It kept me from praying.

"You're such a saint, Janeen!" "You have been such a courageous martyr!" "You know…we got together and made this crown, scepter, and robe of many colors just for you. Our She-Ro!"

Boy, was this coronation wonderful! Ah, to be lifted to such heights and lofty places in front of men. But, oh, the depths of the fall to come.

During the early stages of the decline that eventually ended in divorce in my first marriage, I gave people the power to crown me. I was after anything to soothe my hurt and pain, including power—real or imagined. That is what I wanted—a solution to all my problems that came from the *outside*.

When I allow people to lift me up it is only a matter of time before they will let me down. I will fall because when I let others lift me up it creates a situation in which I will forever feel indebted to them for the "lift." The fatigue of never measuring up to their whims alone will cause me to fall, maybe even jump. Or I will fall because they can arbitrarily exercise the power they hold and snatch the pedestal from underneath me, seeing as they are the ones with all the power.

I knew that the fall was inevitable, but I stashed that thought way on the back shelf. The "lift" is what I wanted, and I gravitated towards anything that reinforced it. My desire for vindication during the time before my divorce was final was the open door to the enemy's influence over my thought life. I liken it to the following thought:

I wanted to sway in the wind like the fronds of a palm tree high up in the sky, close to the sun. Towering over "lowly" brambles, getting a lot of attention, waving to passersby with the passion of the wind by the seashore. Of course, I was a bramble, too, but I allowed my fair-weather comrades to make me think my leafless skinny twigs were palm fronds. Their flattery just provided for my ego to "lift" me to the heights I needed to make my "super twig" tale complete.

Silly, isn't it?

After a great deal of pain and stress, I had to acknowledge my sinful, pride-hungry nature and drag it under subjection to the rule of Christ's Spirit and His Word.

> *"This is the verdict: Light has come into the world, but men loved darkness instead of light because their deeds were evil. Everyone who does evil hates the light, and will not come into the light for fear that his deeds will be exposed. But whoever lives by the truth comes into the light, so that it may be seen plainly that what he has done has been done through God."*
>
> *(John 3:19-21 NIV)*

My flesh predisposes me or inclines me to not see the light. My flesh also predisposes me to desire a high place. At certain times the temptation is greater than at others. Nonetheless, in order to not fall into a dark realm I have to remain on my face before the Father to keep His perspective and vision in clear view.

Isn't it something how so often it seems to be such little things that make great men fall?

> *"Pride goes before destruction, a haughty spirit before a fall."*
>
> *(Proverbs 16:18 NIV)*

Well P-R-I-D-E is only five letters, but it is no little thing!

I have allowed people to do that to me and even permitted others to believe that big "super twig" lie about themselves. I have participated in giving a "lift" to another person a time or two, too. Flattery is just a fancy lie that still resides in the lowest class— SIN.

I was willing to participate in and believe I was a martyr in my marriage while adamantly overlooking that there were two sides to my story. The years of enabling did make me culpable along with some other sin *ish-you's* I had.

Those who were rallying to "lift" me were all-too-willing to spoon-feed me my own poisonous "me-the-martyr" version of events. But in time they got tired of holding me up with that lie.

As the reality of the responsibilities of caring for three children and the toll of grieving began weighing on me heavily, they kicked the pedestal from underneath me and confiscated the crown, scepter, and robe they had bestowed upon me. So I had some work to do. I had to provide shade, recycle the air around me, and shelter my three little chicks.

The choice about how to handle the hardballs life threw my way were mine alone. The Bible speaks about this in James, where he cautions that when we are tempted we should not think that we are tempted of the Lord. My temptation was my own lust. It doesn't matter who was pushing or pulling me or shouting at me to "swing that bat," I played the pitches according to what was in my heart.

Sometimes I consulted with God, sometimes I didn't. Sometimes I played the Godly pitches, and sometimes I let them pass.

I am responsible for my own actions.

There was never a time when I was unable to choose differently which of the pitches I took or let pass. It is tempting to say that God brought hard times my way. He didn't bring them my way but He did allow them.

> *"Where can I go from your Spirit? Where can I flee from your presence? If I go up to the heavens, you are there; if I make my bed in the depths, you are there. If I rise on the wings of the dawn, if I settle on the far side of the sea, even there your hand will guide me, your right hand will hold me fast. If I say, 'Surely the darkness will hide me and the light become night around me,' even the darkness will not be dark to you; the night will shine like the day, for darkness is as light to you. For you created my inmost being; you knit me together in my mother's womb. I praise you because I am fearfully and wonderfully made; your works are wonderful, I know that full well."*
>
> (Psalm 139:7-14 NIV)

I knew that God's best for my life was more peaceful than it had become. The cruel demands of serving worthless idols sorely disrupted even the thought of being in complete peace.

God tells us how to gain liberty from the bondage of hanging onto worthless idols. Let go of them all, then grab tightly onto Him!

> *"See, I set before you today life and prosperity, death and destruction. For I command you today to love the*

LORD your God, to walk in his ways, and to keep his
commands, decrees and laws; then you will live and
increase, and the LORD your God will bless you in the
land you are entering to possess. But if your heart turns
away and you are not obedient, and if you are drawn
away to bow down to other gods and worship them, I
declare to you this day that you will certainly be
destroyed. You will not live long in the land you are
crossing the Jordan to enter and possess. This day I call
heaven and earth as witnesses against you that I have
set before you life and death, blessings and curses. Now
choose life, so that you and your children may live and
that you may love the LORD your God, listen to his
voice, and hold fast to him. For the LORD is your life,
and he will give you many years in the land he swore to
give to your fathers, Abraham, Isaac and Jacob."
(Deuteronomy 30:15-20 NIV)

Choose to and then let the idols go!

Dethroning my idols and letting go was what I did in the
belly of this great oceanliner. Perhaps a submarine is a better met-
aphor of my great fish. Surely my "out of this world" oceanic fac-
tors assisted in fortifying my resolve to obey God and let them all
go. In addition to that (and more obvious than ever) was the fact
that no one was able to deliver and care for me now.

Only the True God was able to accomplish such a miraculous feat and deliver me out of this deep.

Sometimes dethroning idols is a quick act, and sometimes it
is achieved through a more laborious process. Some idols can be
swatted to the floor like an irritating mosquito. With others, you
may need to erect scaffolding to get up high enough to plant the
bombs needed to blow them up.

All my idols were made of the same materials as my millstone. Many didn't survive my jump into the crashing waves.

Extirpated.

They were uprooted and flung off me into clear view. After seeing them in the magnified light of the water with all of their gross detail, I decided not to offer them a piggyback ride to shore. Besides, dead things are much heavier to carry and my attempt to be pleasing and provide a smooth ride would have drowned me.

Still other idols gave way under the crushing pressure of my descent to the belly of the earth.

Asphyxiated.

I had no desire to reach out and help these idols or to provide these leech types the protection my inner body would have given them. Besides, doing so would require me to join them in their lifeless ascent to the surface of the ocean.

I was absolutely thrilled with my increasingly lightened load. The surgery was a success!

Thank God I finally jumped!

This was the most tedious and intricate pathway. The needs I described here were a few of the many that I served as "my way" to satisfy my longing heart. The tediousness and intricacies were due to the requirement to consciously engage my will to rid these habits and behaviors. I couldn't cry foul or victim when I was standing at the open door of deliverance and was able but would not walk through it!

Thank God I was ejected out of the belly of my great fish right through the open door on the seashore. Yet, though I had been moving forward and making progress, there was an element of power to push through that was still *noisily absent*.

CHAPTER 6

Spit Up Ashore

*"When my life was ebbing away, I remembered you,
LORD, and my prayer rose to you, to your holy temple.
Those who cling to worthless idols forfeit the grace that
could be theirs. But I, with a song of thanksgiving, will
sacrifice to you. What I have vowed I will make good.
Salvation comes from the LORD. And the LORD com-
manded the fish, and it vomited Jonah onto dry land."*
(Jonah 2:7-10 NIV)

HEY, DO YOU KNOW how to walk inconspicuously down the
street covered in vomit? I couldn't seem to get that right. More se-
riously, though, when my darkness was dispelled from my life, it
was noticeable. As I sat on that shore, others just silently stared in
great anticipation of what I would do next, pondering my soiled
condition. There were some whom I considered "close" who saw
me and ran away from me crying, "Ugh!"

My condition was altered because I had been enveloped by
the Lord. Consecrated. It was noticeable. The first evidence of
this newness to others was when my desire and will to be a pleasing whiff of sweetness to them changed. Gone, too, was my drive
to make them feel comfortable around "the new" me. My condition was now a sweet scent to the Lord, and that is really all that
mattered. Uprightness before God is not always pleasing to the
human senses. All in all, I had been through too much with my

gracious Lord and I was not going to deny Him now through my attempts to please finite humans.

The passage above is my favorite in the book of Jonah. It sums up by identifying: what got me to the Light of Love and uncovered my darkness; that clinging to Christ is the key to keeping me in the Light of Love; that maintaining spiritual disciplines allows me to show others to the Light of Love; and that stirring up my gifts sustains me when the dark clouds come.

Though I had been moving forward and was making progress, I did not gain access to the element of power to propel me to the end of my journey until I invited and asked God to help me see it "His way." *I prayed.*

> *"When my life was ebbing away, I remembered you, LORD, and my prayer rose to you, to your holy temple."*
>
> *(Jonah 2:7 NIV)*

Communicate, Communicate, Communicate

Consecrated prayer is what provided sufficient pressure to force out the remaining *ish-you's* contributing to my blindness. Their removal uncovered my remaining darkness and ushered in the Light. Consecrated time in prayer was the foundational practice that purged me of my *ish-you's*. Idolatry kept me from prayer and the delivering and healing presence of God I needed to free me from the snares of the idols I was worshipping. It kept me from seeking God continually as I relied on "my way" for things I should have been relying on God to provide for me. God heard every rudimentary prayer I offered to Him as holy, but in order to keep the Light shining continually, I needed to pray continually, while abiding in His presence.

Through prayer I got to know God. He was so much more than the "Great Almighty Judge." Though as His child I am to respect him, I learned that I had no need to be afraid of Him. What had kept me from achieving this level of connectivity and clarity was my sin. Through this discipline of consecrated prayer I grew to know Him as the Great Physician with very gentle healing hands.

The hospital event I recalled in chapter one, the isolation in the belly of the great fish, and all that transpired between those pathways contributed to the early development of my prayer life, but the discipline of prayer came about as a result of the consecrated time I had talking with God in the belly of the great fish. My loneliness led me to obey the command to pray without ceasing (I Thessalonians 5:17).

Prayer is simply having a conversation with God—talking and listening, sometimes both and sometimes just one or the other. God's language is holy, and the more I mastered it the better I was able to understand Him because the problem was never that He didn't understand me.

There is a lot of talk these days about "praying the Word of God back to Him." It makes sense because His language *is* His Word. If that phrase is a little too "churchy" for you, as it was for me, the following example might help you to understand it better (as it did for me).

I took Spanish in high school and college. My instructors could always understand me when I spoke in English or Spanish because they spoke and understood both. They were bilingual. The problem early on was that I could not understand them when they spoke Spanish for the simple reason that I did not know Spanish. But the more I studied it, I understood it, and could communicate with them much better.

And though prayer is similar in that it is not my native language, God, the Author, can always understand me and get His message across because He made the very place where my capacity to pray is seated—in my *heart*, not in my brain.

Being able to communicate in God's language required that I study it. I even purchased flash cards as many people do when learning a new language; in this case, the flash cards were scripture memory verse cards. The more I studied His Words, the more I understood Him when He spoke to me and the better I could identify His voice speaking to me in the midst of the circus noise around me. Before I was ejected from the belly of the fish, I had an experience in prayer similar to many I had witnessed during my adolescent church years. I called it a "soul pouring."

Soul Pouring

For me "Soul Pouring" was the one movement in the Sunday service that scared the devil out of me. This "movement" in my church's tradition was actually called "The Altar Call."

This was a movement in the service when the deacons would turn toward the altar in the front of the church as congregants would gather behind them around the altar and kneel down and begin what I thought was a frightening incantation to summon the spirits from beyond and awaken the dead. They would be moaning, praying, crying, and singing all at the same time.

During this time, there was one song they always sang that nailed my fear on the head and my fanny to the pew (or, when I was younger, to my mama's lap). I have no idea what the actual title of the hymn was or the name of the genius who wrote it, but it was a call-and-response style delivery in which everyone over the age of 30 would participate. The song would start out with the lyric, "I Love the Lord, He heard my cry," and without fail before the leading deacon finished that line, people would start shouting, screaming, wailing, and crying aloud all over the sanctuary.

Granted, other mines of demonstrative expression detonated throughout the service such as when the tenor section sang their chorus part alone followed by the sopranos' hitting the high note and the pastor beginning to whoop. But my goal each Sunday morning was not to be around during the "soul pouring." I'd go so far as to even try to cause my family to be too late to get there in time for it. That explosion left me undone, everytime. It was wild!

I was just a little girl and didn't have too much "theology," but I could *feel!* This soul pouring movement seemed always to usher in the manifest presence of the living God, and it was His presence that scared me to death because it was so overwhelmingly awesome. I was not used to such an emotional tugging on my heart and I didn't like it. Just being in His presence, whether I was participating in the "soul pouring" or not, yanked on my heart strings.

His presence was truly awesome! My feeling of being overwhelmed was enhanced by the actions of those who were participating in the soul pouring. As they cried out to the Lord, it was as if all of their hopes, dreams, *ish-you's*, oppressions, hurts, dismays, and disappointments poured out like a blood sacrifice described in the Old Testament. I could feel their faith in God's capacity to Love them through it all and in His manifest presence as they enveloped and soaked it all up. As I mentioned earlier, my family was not the "touchy-feely" kind, but there was something about the manifest presence of God that provided an "exhale" for burdens that a mask couldn't stand in the presence of! Standing or sitting in His presence was a critical lifeline for those particpants. I could not understand it as a child, but I certainly could feel it, and at this point in my life "soul pouring" is a critical lifeline for *me*.

No giant multimedia screens, no band, no accompaniment tracks, no world-renowned musician, soloist, choir, group, or clinician could teach me what this time of worship did for me. It taught me how to cry out to God with my whole being, for myself and by myself, in spirit and in truth, while basking in His manifest presence.

> *"God is a Spirit: and they that worship him must worship him in spirit and in truth."*
>
> *(John 4:24 KJV)*

As I grew in my relationship with the Lord and communicated better with Him my prayer life became more structured, but "soul pouring" will forever be a part of my prayer life with God. Along with the components of the Lord's Prayer (Matthew 6:9-13) and the 23rd Psalm, I use the following popular acronym to help keep my prayers balanced. I am not certain whom to credit for it, but it has served me very well: A.C.T.S.I.—Adoration, Confession, Thanksgiving, Supplication, and Intercession.

There are great books on prayer that touch on one or more components I have outlined in the acronym, but I want to share elements that I gleaned along my journey. I will briefly touch on each one, but I gleaned the most from the fields of confession, supplication, and intercession. Before I begin to detail this prayer model I use, I want to stress that it is not a formula for knowing God intimately.

Adoration

Adoration means *to reverence* or *pay homage to*. It is an outward display. The Jewish custom for showing adoration was to put off their shoes or lie prostrate. It is interesting to note that the word *adore* does not appear in the King James Version of the Bible, though the behavior appears throughout.

Though while I am driving in the car I cannot lie prostrate, I often do so during my quiet time at home. Doing so impacts my perspective by focusing on God's holiness. Practicing this A. component of the prayer model helps me maintain a reverent attitude while carrying out the C.S.T.I. The disciplines of tithing and fasting fit here for me, too, as outward displays of how I adore the Lord and desire to stay intimately near Him.

Confession

Confession means *to openly acknowledge sins committed against God or another person(s)*. To properly confess requires humility, faith, and meekness. Humility enables me to adore the Lord in worship and pour my soul out in His presence freely enough for true confession to take place. I must submit my will to the Lord in order to genuinely confess, but I cannot do so without faith. As P. B. Wilson states in her book *Liberated Through Submission*, the ultimate paradox is that:

"Submission without faith is slavery."

Submission does not mean subjection to others. It means a demonstrated trust in a trustworthy God. (Meekness is another requirement for properly confessing to God, but my learning of meekness is another story altogether.)

Meek Bubbles

When I was a little girl growing up in sunny southern California, I learned a song during Christmastime. Although it was great entertainment for me, it utterly disgusted my mother. The song started with: "Jingle Bells, Batman smells, Robin laid an egg..."

Do you remember that desecrated version of an otherwise joyous Christmas jingle?

Anyway, my mother told me not to sing that "filthy" song anymore. Much as I tried not to sing it, I continued. It was no mystery why I continued to sing it. I simply didn't want to submit to her control.

My mom promised me that if I sang that song again, she would wash my mouth out with soap. Well, even though I believed her, I sang it again. In her shock at my obstinate belting of this tune again, she looked at my dad in utter amazement. She asked me why I would sing the song again knowing what my disobedience would bring. I told her, "I don't know."

Perhaps suspecting that I was suffering a bout of temporary insanity, she let me "slide." She restated her promise to me, but again I had the stubborn gumption to sing *that* song!

I tried to place my hand over my mouth and stop the sound melodiously flowing out of my face, but it didn't work. She looked at my dad in amazement again! She promised that her patience would only allow for this last "accident," but that was it. If I dared sing it again, she would not only wash my mouth out with soap but spank my little bottom.

Well, it was quiet for a few tense moments and then, all of a sudden, to everyone's surprise, out came *Jingle Smells* again. Frankly, I had no desire to bring my choice of singing that song under her control. I made a dashing attempt to cover my mouth, but it came a little too late. As promised, I was escorted to the restroom and received the promised mouth full of soap and the spanking. I must say that she appropriately applied the board of education to my seat of knowledge.

The point was that I learned the high importance and value of a meek spirit. What is a meek spirit? Anne Ortlund says in her book *Disciplines of a Beautiful Woman:*

"Meekness is not weakness. Meekness is strength under control."

This topic provides a segue to an issue I ever keep before the Lord with regard to confession—*my mouth!*

Life and death are in power of the tongue (Proverbs 18:21), so it is a biggie and not to be regarded casually. God hates a lying tongue, gossip, and slander, and look at His response to murmurers.

"And do not grumble, as some of them did—and were killed by the destroying angel."
(1 Corinthians 10:10 NIV)

"Nor complain, as some of them also complained, and were destroyed by the destroyer."
(1 Corinthians 10:10 NKJV)

"Neither murmur ye, as some of them also murmured, and were destroyed of the destroyer."
(1 Corinthians 10:10 KJV)

I took the liberty of citing this scripture in three versions of the Bible so there would be little confusion about God's response to these mummerers—namely: *death.*

In the military and other places of employment, service, or duty, such a repiner can be fired on the grounds of mouthiness, AKA insubordination! Shouldn't members of God's army be dealt with at least as harshly as this? Yes. But I am so thankful that He is slow to anger and full of mercy!

Another lesson about how critical the mouth is and how God regards it came as I sat watching a cartoon about Joshua and the battle at Jericho with my children. The thought that kept going through my mind as I watched the film was...*I bet the enemy soldiers and maybe other onlookers standing watch atop the walls of Jericho spat on Joshua and the children of Israel as they obediently marched around the walls silently. Possibly they hurled insults and even more than that.*

If I had been marching in their number, it would have been really hard for me to get up and do it again the next day, after day, after day, quietly! Negative and critical speech is infectious, isn't it? Great was the temptation in the midst of the insults and spitballs to feel mad, humiliated, and abandoned by God as well as to question His wisdom and His leadership choices.

The fact that they submitted their tongues to God's command to keep silent opened my eyes to see. All they had to throw at the wall was the faithful promise that the Lord gave them (Joshua 6:2-5). At the end of the day that is all I have as His child, though I still have to march around the wall. It was not because of any good that they did but solely God's faithfulness that secured this victory for the children of Israel.

Perhaps in their silence they saw their pride and need to trust and obey God more as the walls tumbled. All in all, everyone saw the result of obeying God—prevailing over obstacles.

> *"May the words of my mouth and the meditation of my heart be pleasing in your sight, O Lord, my Rock and my Redeemer.*
>
> *(Psalm 19:14 NIV)*

Thankfulness

Thankfulness means *to be aware and appreciative of an advantage given.* Believers in Jesus Christ are commanded as follows:

> *"Give thanks in all circumstances, for this is God's will for you in Christ Jesus." (1 Thessalonians 5:18 NIV)*

This does not mean that I should celebrate adversity, evil, and other ills or be satisfied with them. Neither is this thankfulness that God commands born of comparing my struggles with those of others. It is not being thankful because "I don't have it as bad as they do." "Comparison is carnality," I once heard a great preacher say. My thankfulness is to be born out of my time walking with the Lord be it in good times or bad times.

I have learned to see each tough pathway along the journey as just *one* pathway, not the whole course of my journey. I was just passing through it to the next one with the Lord. The same is true when I was tempted to pitch a tent on one of the "fun" and "easygoing" legs of the journey.

God has proven to me that each step I take with Him has a purpose that is for my greater good. God has not left me or ever "let me down." He never has! He is always with me.

> *"Every word of God is flawless; he is a shield to those who take refuge in him."*
>
> *(Proverbs 30:5 NIV)*

It is also a discipline to maintain a thankful perspective "in" everything. But as long as I remember that I am going through with the Lord then I will be able to sacrificially offer up thanksgiving to God even when it doesn't feel good.

Supplication

Supplication means *to humbly and earnestly ask for something.* What enables us to make proper requests to God?

> *"But seek first His kingdom and His righteousness, and all these things will be given to you as well."*
>
> *(Matthew 6:33 NIV)*

Proper requests flow out of the heart whose priority is seeking the kingdom of God and His righteousness. As I said before, there are many great books on prayer. In chapter 13 ("God Speaks Through Prayer") of *Experiencing God*, Blackaby and King touch on the issue of when you pray for one thing and get another, when God is silent, and much more. I highly recommend this book.

To Work or Not to Work

When I was in college before I married, I worked, lived in my own apartment, and paid my own bills. I was leading a relatively responsible young adult life. I didn't finish college and got married. My first husband and I agreed on the importance of my staying home with the children, at least until they began school. Financially it also made sense, seeing that most of the money I would have earned at the time would have gone to childcare costs.

On the surface, it all looked so good, but underneath was a neglectful shame. I remember a church member seeing a huge blown-out hole in my pantyhose that my suit skirt couldn't cover up. Once a minister's wife scolded me about the need for me to brush my daughter's "nappy hair." She didn't know and probably wouldn't have believed that I did not have a brush for her soft hair, so I had been gathering it into a pigtail to the best of my ability. They just couldn't imagine that I had no financial resources to purchase needed panty hose or a hairbrush.

His neglect of the children and me led to more daily drama and stress than I care to recall. This behavior was magnified with children.

While I was working my fanny off as a homemaker, I constantly felt as though I had to approach him with my needs apologetically because I did not have any income. There was plenty of money coming into the house, but he often reminded me by his words and, more often, by his behavior that it was not my money.

His greatest leverage over me was that I lacked my own access to and control of finances. It had always been effective in keeping me "in line" and "under control." Neglect was a powerful weapon used on me to make me feel as though I had no rights and no voice to ask for what the children or I needed.

I was so often deprived of the most basic practical needs that I felt as though I had "nothing!" I tried to earn money through the entrepreneurial ventures (as I mentioned before), but to no avail. He would often have last-minute changes of heart that forced me to take the children with me to board meetings of the non-profit I founded. I had even taken them with me to clean the house of a wealthy family I was working for.

I had no real viable options for working outside the home because there weren't any positions that would allow me to take the children with me.

I was stuck! But as I recalled in chapter three, as I began to demonstrate my trust in God, the more I could see that He was more than able to provide for my needs. The point here is that there is nothing wrong or shameful in asking for material needs to be met. I was on the extreme side where I didn't ask for the things I needed because I thought doing so was carnal and ungodly. More bad theology I had ingested somewhere in my development. On the other extreme, my heart is so burdened for so many in my generation who are pursuing what they see as material things in God's hands and not His heart.

> *"No one can serve two masters. Either he will hate the one and love the other, or he will be devoted to the one and despise the other. You cannot serve both God and Money. Therefore I tell you, do not worry about your*

life, what you will eat or drink; or about your body, what you will wear. Is not life more important than food, and the body more important than clothes? Look at the birds of the air; they do not sow or reap or store away in barns, and yet your heavenly Father feeds them. Are you not much more valuable than they? Who of you by worrying can add a single hour to his life? And why do you worry about clothes? See how the lilies of the field grow. They do not labor or spin. Yet I tell you that not even Solomon in all his splendor was dressed like one of these. If that is how God clothes the grass of the field, which is here today and tomorrow is thrown into the fire, will he not much more clothe you, O you of little faith? So do not worry, saying, 'What shall we eat?' or 'What shall we drink?' or 'What shall we wear?' For the pagans run after all these things, and your heavenly Father knows that you need them. But seek first his kingdom and his righteousness, and all these things will be given to you as well. Therefore do not worry about tomorrow, for tomorrow will worry about itself. Each day has enough trouble of its own."

(Matthew 6:24-34 NIV)

Intercession

Intercession means to *petition in favor of another; to go between two parties in an effort to reconcile differences*. What a privilege to be able to advocate on behalf of another before the True and Living God. It is my duty and privilege as a child of God to take the needs and concerns of others before God and petition Him on their behalf. Though in most cases, more steps are required, intercession is one of the most powerful steps in serving others. This is the area of my prayer life the enemy tries hardest to stifle. This other-centered discipline is a challenge for many in our self-centered culture.

You've probably heard it said, "Good help sure is hard to find." Well I pray that when I get to heaven's gates God doesn't take one look at me and say that. Hopefully He will say, "Good and faithful servant, well done."

After the divorce, the most impressive lesson of servanthood came when there was no laundry or dish detergent in the household. All the laundry and dishes needed to be done and all there was was bar soap. Mind you, in college I had washed laundry and even dishes in shampoo, but to my dismay, neither was available! What an inconvenience!

Even though I had given my tithes and offering, provision wasn't the way I desired or the way I expected. What I did have was bar soap. Honestly, I felt as though I had been gyped. There were no resources to do anything other than begin the arduous task of reducing the bar of soap into the kitchen sink and the washing machine for use.

There was a time when bar soap served a multi-purpose. I remember one of the rare times I went to the grocery store with my maternal grandmother and she shared with me about an "old school" bar soap that was multi-purpose. She claimed this soap could treat poison ivy, rid plants of pests, rid pets of ticks and fleas, remedy black spot fungus in roses, and do a fine job on the laundry, to boot. Even though I tried to shift my attitude with this recollection, I was still in a funk.

To serve is to be used, and praying for my enemies is still a tough thing. Though I was hesitant to allow myself to be vulnerable for use it was through serving others within the boundaries God assigned that I got free to serve again. I was no longer owned by the fear of being "used all up," and I no longer resented the sense of inconvenience that often comes with serving.

My children didn't deserve to go to school in dirty socks and underwear. So I humbled myself and with a meek spirit submersed my arms elbow-deep in the washing machine water and reduced the bar of bath soap to prevent them from having to go to school in dirty clothes. In faith I knew a better day was ahead. I just needed to be obedient and faithful to God towards both my loved ones and my enemies.

I had been commissioned to be God's servant. My commitment and obedience to God did not endow me with the "boss's power and authority." Just because I contribute to the bottom line, it does not mean that I am the owner. I am a servant!

God has an infinite supply. When I am called to render service to others as unto Him, He has already built in boundaries for my protection. I cannot be used up when the mission to serve is God-ordained because it is my serving through Him that allows for my unlimited supply.

> *"I have no need of a bull from your stall or of goats from your pens, for every animal of the forest is mine, and the cattle on a thousand hills. I know every bird in the mountains, and the creatures of the field are mine. If I were hungry I would not tell you, for the world is mine, and all that is in it. Do I eat the flesh of bulls or drink the blood of goats? Sacrifice thank offerings to God, fulfill your vows to the Most High, and call upon me in the day of trouble; I will deliver you, and you will honor me."*
>
> *(Psalm 50:9-15 NIV)*

Forgive

Because of the faithfulness of one many are saved. Jonah's service helped save the Ninevites, Noah's service secured the future of humankind, and Christ's service saved us all for eternity! The list of biblical models of Godly servanthood goes on and on. I pray that my service to my family will preserve a Godly legacy for generations to come.

I am no savior, but I do desire to be an obedient servant so that, as a result of my service to God, many will benefit.

The side-effects of serving can be downright "stinky." Surely the whale vomit on Jonah was foul-smelling not to mention unsightly. Consider Noah's faithfulness and the condition of the ark after 40 days and 40 nights with an arkful of livestock. The horror of the Jesus' crucifixion defies adequate description and serves as a reminder of two things: (1) As a result of my service to others, I may need to forgive, and (2) In the course of my service I may have to embrace what I call "Gethsemane Strength" to empower me to press through.

In his book *The Gift of Forgiveness*, Dr. Charles Stanley explains that the cycle of forgiveness begins when an offense is committed, a debt is owed, and the forgiveness is the cancellation of that debt. Unforgiveness is cruel. It forces the offended to carry around something that is dead, gone, and in the past. This is similar to one type of torturous punishment to which murderers in ancient times were sentenced....

A person convicted of murder had to bear the body of his victim affixed in some fashion to his own body and had to carry that body around with him. As the body of the victim decayed and became infested with maggots, mites, etc, it infected the murderer as well and caused him to die an agonizing, slow, horrible death.

The spirit of unforgiveness is a lot like that. As you lug around offenses, they becomes toxic and infest your being. You can only pretend for so long that you are not being affected and infected by the dead thing you are lugging around before you begin to reek of toxicity so much that people run the other way when they see you coming. "Stinky!" they scream. Their response can create even more bitterness in one walking in unforgiveness. What the unforgiven and the unforgiving need is an intercessor.

It is true that, though you maintain a spirit of forgiveness toward your offender, reconciliation will not occur until they repent.

During my old "do-bot" days, I participated in many lies. I kept up the appearance that genuine repentance had occurred by enabling a harmonious existence on the surface. All the while I felt as though I was rotting to death on the inside. My effort to "fix" things by keeping the tide calm created an unmanageable distance in which the enemy thrived. My enabling also allowed a looming awkwardness to prevail that bred frustratation because I was affirming a lie.

I so desperately wanted things to be "okay" that I had to reach outside of myself to stop the habit of affirming lies. I had to employ that "Gethsemane Strength." Gethesamane Strength muscles around my flesh and consciously subjects it to my spirit man, instead of the other way around.

Gethsemane Strength
I found no evidence in scripture that Christ ever struggled with affirming lies, but He did struggle with aligning His will to the Father's. He was victorious in accomplishing the alignment (Luke 22:42).

It is often difficult to submit our will to the "call of God" on our life when the pathway ahead is certain to be unpleasant! Why? Because obeying His will will surely cost us more than our flesh is willing to pay. Our flesh is strong and desires to drive our spirit with its own selfish desires!

> *"I say, live by the Spirit, and you will not gratify the desires of the sinful nature. For the sinful nature desires what is contrary to the Spirit, and the Spirit what is contrary to the sinful nature. They are in conflict with each other, so that you do not do what you want."*
>
> *(Galatians 5:16-17 KJV)*

We have to get supernatural endowment to empower our spirit to succeed over our flesh and submit to the pathway that Christ has for us. That endowment comes through our obedient action.

Look at Jesus! He struggled in the Garden of Gethsemane to align His flesh with His spirit.

> *"Then Jesus went with his disciples to a place called Gethsemane, and he said to them, Sit here while I go over there and pray.' He took Peter and the two sons of Zebedee along with him, and he began to be sorrowful and troubled. Then he said to them, 'My soul is overwhelmed with sorrow to the point of death. Stay here and keep watch with me.' Going a little farther, he fell with his face to the ground and prayed, 'My Father, if it is possible, may this cup be taken from me. Yet not as I will, but as you will.' Then he returned to his disciples and found them sleeping. 'Could you men not keep watch with me for one hour?' he asked Peter. 'Watch and pray so that you will not fall into temptation. The spirit is willing, but the body is weak.'*

> *He went away a second time and prayed, 'My Father,*
> *if it is not possible for this cup to be taken away unless I*
> *drink it, may your will be done.'"*
>
> *(Matthew 26:36-42 NIV)*

He struggled to align His flesh with His spirit, but get this: The fact that Jesus, being sinless, struggled to align His flesh with His spirit proves that to struggle with this is *not* sin! He was both fully God and fully man and thus set the perfect example of our ability to overcome the struggle to align our flesh through obedient action.

> *"During the days of Jesus' life on earth, he offered up*
> *prayers and petitions with loud cries and tears to the*
> *one who could save him from death, and he was heard*
> *because of his reverent submission."*
>
> *(Hebrews 5:7 NIV)*

That's what Gethsemane strength is all about—*reverent submission*. I am enabled with the power to prevail in this capacity when I look beyond me and my struggle as Jesus did.

> *"Let us fix our eyes on Jesus, the author and perfecter of*
> *our faith, who for the joy set before him endured the*
> *cross, scorning its shame, and sat down at the right*
> *hand of the throne of God."*
>
> *(Hebrews 12:2 NIV)*

When I consider my children and their future, it gives me vision beyond my struggle. When I think of my heavenly home and Christ's love for me, I gain the strength to press through those struggles.

Discovering a new prayer life through God's grace uncovered my darkness and exposed my heart to the rays of the Light of Love that I had been craving and longing for. As I reflect on it, it all seems (and must sound) simple enough. I can recall how my mother used to warn me, when I was meeting a new kid in school or in the neighborhood, "Janeen, don't make such a rash judgment. Talk to them and get to know them first."

I had made my pursuit much more complex than it needed to be. God was not some lofty ethereal indifferent entity; He was my Heavenly Father. He was not a preoccupied parent; He was my attentive Shepherd. He was my Great Physician whose gentle nail-scarred hands longed to heal and embrace me every moment of every day. All I needed was to have a conversation with Him—to get to know Him without making a rash judgment. He was standing by waiting and longing for me to trust Him and disrobe in His presence to share in intimate fellowship. He had already given me all of Him. I didn't even have to know what to say in His presence…I just needed to get there.

> *"Likewise the Spirit also helpeth our infirmities: for we know not what we should pray for as we ought: but the Spirit itself maketh intercession for us with groanings which cannot be uttered."*
>
> *(Romans 8:26 NIV)*

I allowed Him to take my hand in His and to lead me moment by moment into a deeper more intimate relationship with Him. As I cling to Christ it keeps me daily in the Light of His Love and grace. *Oh for grace to trust Him more.*

CHAPTER 7

Cling & Sing

AFTER MY DARKNESS was uncovered and I was found in the presence of the Light of Love, I wanted to stay and be kept there. The key for me to do this was found in the following verse:

> *"Those who cling to worthless idols forfeit the grace that could be theirs."*

(Jonah 2:8)

When I cling to Christ, I retain the grace that could be mine. To cling means *to refuse to give something up; to hold onto someone or something tightly.* How do I cling to Christ? By obeying the Father's directives through the model of Christ.

Clinging is not a passive activity. It is aggressive. Think of a child who wants to be picked up clinging to his mommy's knee with unyielding tears. When my children would get exhausted and demand that I pick them up, I could have probably walked around the whole house with them attached to my leg. Through each bumpy step, they would keep clinging until I picked them up and carried them. This is the manner of clinging to Christ that keeps me in the Light of Love.

Imitate Christ

"Fake it till you make it" is probably the worst advice floating around out there today. I am not certain whom to credit for this gem of pop psychology.

Better counsel is to prepare for the season you hope for. Don't fake it, pretending that the season already exists. That is presumption, and presumption is *not* faith. Faith is what pleases God. Presumption is as foolish as wearing a full-length mink coat to lunch in August in sunny southern California as if it were winter in New England. It is sorely out of order and can cause injury—in the case of the spirit, it can cause a Son-stroke of disappointment and discouragement.

I remember practicing gymnastics for hours at a club that has produced, to date, at least two Olympic-caliber athletes. There is an uneven bars combination skill called a "glide kip." A glide is when you simply hold onto the bar and swing your suspended body in a fluid forward motion. A kip is when you pull your body up atop the bar, in one motion, as you begin the swing backwards out of the glide move.

"Steve," as I shall refer to him, was one of my coaches at the Charter Oak Gymnastics Club, and on this particular evening I was practicing like a mad woman trying to get that skill. Steve came over and tried to show me that getting this skill combination was kind of like pulling up a pair of pants while getting dressed. Easy for him to say! I was so frustrated that I couldn't get it. He made it sound so simple!

I tried to tell myself that it was only hard because I was attempting it in a pike position rather than a straddled one. But that wasn't why (for those of you not familiar with gymnastics, bear with me for just a moment). The problem was that my technique was wrong.

I don't know whether it was sweat or tears in my eyes, but all I could see was red!

Steve yelled over to me and said, "Janeen, it's just like pulling up a pair of pants."

I tried hard to imagine that as I attempted the combination over and over again. The palms of my hands were shredded to bits from the friction of the uneven bars. Chalk was all over me. Steve could tell I was exhausted because he teased me a little at the break in my form as I began to kick and wiggle in a desperate attempt to get my hips on top of that bar.

Anyway, Steve walked over and told me to go get some water. I didn't want to. I wanted to get that skill. But he insisted that I immediately stop and get a drink of water! That made me even madder!

"Practice makes perfect," I told him, my tone sharp, "and I gotta practice to get this now!" Then he said something to me that has proven such a valuable nugget of wisdom. "Janeen," he said, "practice makes *habits*. If you practice it wrong, it will take more time to learn it the right way."

That was the best drink of cold water I had ever had, and I got the skill down before I left that night. I apply that nugget of wisdom in my pursuit of being Christ-like. Practice makes habits—not perfection. Imitating Christ could not be accomplished by my doing what I thought was right or what I thought it looked like, but only by accepting and obeying instruction on what was the correct way. This process is life-long, but it is not a blind undertaking. I have the Father who tells me how, Christ who has shown me, and the Spirit who helps me do it.

It's the little things. In the story of Jonah it wasn't the great wind (1:4), the sea miraculously ceasing from raging (1:15), the great fish swallowing Jonah for three days and nights (1:17), the fish vomiting Jonah upon dry land (2:10), the barbarians having faith in God (3:5), nor the great gourd tree God provided to shade Jonah in the desert; it was the little crimson worm (4:10) that was the straw that broke the camel's back, rendering such a powerful blow to a hardened heart that knew God.

The Spirit of God is like that. Not that it's a little thing, but the discipline of seeking God properly allows us to hear His still small voice, which is critical to our ability to receive and share in God's love.

> *"The Lord said, 'Go out and stand on the mountain in the presence of the Lord, for the Lord is about to pass by.' Then a great and powerful wind tore the mountains apart and shattered the rocks before the Lord, but the Lord was not in the wind. After the wind there was an earthquake, but the Lord was not in the earthquake. After the earthquake came a fire, but the Lord was not in the fire. And after the fire came a gentle whisper. When Elijah heard it, he pulled his cloak over his face and went out and stood at the mouth of the cave. Then a voice said to him, 'What are you doing here, Elijah?'"*
>
> *(I Kings 19:11-13 NIV)*

As I further researched the crimson worm I came across the following "little" quote from Henry Morris' book titled *Biblical Basis for Modern Science* that is such a big wonder:

> "When the female of the scarlet worm species was ready to give birth to her young, she would attach her body to the trunk of a tree, fixing herself so firmly and permanently that she would never leave again. The eggs deposited beneath her body were thus protected until the larvae were hatched and able to enter their own life cycle. As the mother died, the crimson fluid stained her body and the surrounding wood. From the dead bodies of such female scarlet worms, the commercial scarlet

dyes of antiquity were extracted. What a picture this gives of Christ, dying on the tree, shedding his precious blood that he might 'bring many sons unto glory' (Hebrews 2:10)! He died for us, that we might live through him!"

The Old Mother Nurse

"Even when I am old and gray, do not forsake me, O God, till I declare your power to the next generation, your might to all who are to come."

(Psalm 71:18 NIV)

There were ladies positioned at the back of my childhood church who always wore white. From head to toe, hat to glove, stocking and shoe: white. I knew some of them were "nurses" and I knew others were "mothers." For the most part the "mothers" were older women, and they usually sat up front and the "nurses" wore the nurses' caps. I had a hard time telling them apart because they were all taller than me so I called them all "Old Mother Nurses."

One in particular was very fiery! She was a little thing; short and thin but she had a reputation among the the kids as being "a real big meanie." I can see the face of Ms. Malone to this day. She was my childhood Sunday school teacher and one of the church nurses. She always seemed to sit right behind the section in the back of the church where the youth sat together in silent rebellion. The only time you wouldn't catch the youth huddled together was on the third Sunday, which was Youth Sunday. On Youth Sunday the young adult choir would sing and then they would all be up in the choir loft partying in the name of Jesus.

I absolutely despised (or so I thought) so many of the traditions in my church. One was the use of the hymnbook. I wanted to party as a "little thing" and as "Christendom" was coming into a new style of worship I thought it was only "cool and correct" if you had an overhead projector with songs that had no more than a few lines of lyrics and a cool beat. But no! At my church we still used hymnbooks!

Anyway, Ms. Malone was the type who would come up behind during the singing of one of the stanzas and hand you a hymnal opened to the right page and point to the lyrics as they were being sung. She would insist that you sing along, almost pull your ear as a "mother of the church" would do. She was also like a nurse, though, as she would administer the gross, boring medication, kind of massage your throat till all that "good music" was swallowed down.

I count those hymns as dear to me now, and I miss them. But it wasn't until I was having a really bad day that *It is Well with My Soul* came up and out of me. Shocked my socks off! I was better for ingesting the medication and the bruised ear lobe (kidding about the ear, of course).

What happened to those rich hymns? Did our attention span get too short to be able to digest those rich lyrics? I am concerned about what we sing on Sunday mornings. I am concerned about what we listen to throughout the week. Our attempt to be relevant with our so-called Gospel music in many cases has blurred our message, if there was a clear one about God in the first place.

Before I hop down from my soapbox, I need to also add that one song is just too many to be written in the name of Christianity and have no message in it that Christ Himself would communicate.

Just as Ms. Malone set an example for me, I pray that I will not cower to the trends of the day that cause the truth of the Gospel to be watered down to my children. I hope that I leave them with unadulterated truth of the Gospel whether society calls it relevant or not. It is the Truth that will last, and if I leave my children nothing else, my desire is to leave them the knowledge of Jesus so that they will know Him for themselves. There is no greater gift that will carry them through all the ups and downs they will face as adults with families of their own. I have always told them that it doesn't matter if it is my life or anybody else's life they witness, there are always lessons to be learned—either in what to do or what *not* to do. If Jesus is their Plumbline, they will know the difference.

"But I, with a song of thanksgiving, will sacrifice to you.
What I have vowed I will make good."

(Jonah 2:9 NIV)

The life I live before people is a reflection of the spiritual discipline I maintain or the lack thereof. God's commandments in the Bible aren't for what I naturally do, they are for what I do not naturally do. It doesn't command me to eat or sleep; it doesn't have to. But it does have to command me to love my enemies, bless them that curse me, do good to them that hate me, pray for them that despitefully use me and persecute me (Matthew 5:44).

If you surveyed the physical and spiritual condition of my heart you could rate me as healthy or unhealthy. My body will manifest its natural condition, and my behavior will manifest its spiritual condition. The above scripture identifies a critical key—the discipline of thankful praise and worship to God. Just as most can identify good physical disciplines (exercises) to keep the heart physically healthy, the discipline of thankful worship keeps the heart spiritually healthy.

I currently serve as worship leader in my local church and people see me every Sunday. Ushering others into the Light of Love happens not just as a result of using the musical talents He has given me but chiefly as a result of my personal worship to God. And it is as a result of my personal worship that I can show others to the Light of His Love, whether I am on a concert stage, in a church sanctuary, or at the grocery store.

The healthiest exercise (discipline) I engage myself in, especially when I am in a tough spot, is making a new song of thanksgiving to Him. Doing so aids in my spiritual health because it keeps me sensitive to His voice.

A *Souledy* is a term I use to describe my understanding and demonstration of a "new song." It is a melody that flows from my soul. It is a conscious act of my will that I employ through song to meditate on God. The official definition is:

> *A Souledy—A Melodious ode born out of a sacrificial, thankful, meditative, worshipful, reflective, or contemplative utterance of a soul (immortal component of a human) that is focused or centered on the character, attributes, or traits of one or more Persons of the triune God of Christianity.*

I liken a souledy to prayer and the mighty weapon it is. A souledy flows from the soul unto God. When I first began to lift up these new songs to the Lord I was always toiling at my kitchen sink.

These melodies engages God (Psalm 22:3) in a way that I could feel.

A souledy is a conscious declaration that I make to the Lord. Sometimes it comes through intense communion with Him; at other times it comes when I am engaged in intense spiritual warfare. For example, as I would wash those dishes and feel like a slave I would declare to the enemy that "this is not unique to me." I knew that whatever I had allowed or that God had allowed that was causing my portion to be what it was, I was not some special target. I was a child of the Most High God and the enemy hates us all. It also helped me to recall the scripture to *think it not strange the fiery testing (I Peter 4:12)*...with the hope that patience would indeed one day have her perfect work and that God had not left me even though I felt like it. It was a reaching out to God in faith that, although I didn't feel like He was watching, somehow I knew in my soul that He was near.

I can remember another season of asking God why. I had been trying during this time to get into His presence and nothing—not prayers, a new song, scripture—seemed to get me there. I was so desperate for a touch from Him and I was working to get Him to commune with me. I had fallen into a system and began to expect that if a certain time of day, scripture, or song would get me into His presence it always would—like a formula. I was so discouraged when my system failed. I had gotten away from just coming to Him, as I was, empty and needing to be filled. I had been struggling through the book of Job. The words on the page had just been kind of staring back at me, and when I got to the end I cried out to God, "Why? Lord, why won't You commune with me? I am hurting and I need a touch from You. You are the only strength I have access to and now I think You have turned Your back on helping me."

Of course with that admission the "formula" broke and ushered in the presence of the Lord. I was just crying and moaning again, and this time His response came to me in a lyrical form with a melodic structure.

Can You Tell (Why's Answer)
Can You tell
what I see
I know what You expect from Me
it's okay
though you doubt and fear
I love you, I love you
My Love

When I feel rattled or lost this souledy comes to my heart and I feel comforted. It is not just the song that comforts me but the lessons I gleaned from the book of Job (I was finally able to get through it with more than memorizing what the page looked like). God never forsakes His own, regardless of what we may "feel" like.

He will enable you, too!

Sustain Us

Calvary Strength is what I call the gracious empowerment God provides to His children to obey Him when the heart is willing but the flesh is literally too weak. It is also the chief example to me of Christ's obedience.

As I read over the scriptures detailing the events leading up to the death of Christ at Calvary, I learn about this grace God gives His children to empower us to obey Him. The physical improbability that one human body could have endured what Christ endured on the cross is incredible!

All those lashes with the cat o' nine tails alone should have killed Him, but they didn't. Having a crown of thorns so jagged that it cut into His scalp and possibly even scratched His skull should have made Him too delirious with pain to be aware of

His surroundings. But it didn't. The stress (*hematohydrosis*) and certain dehydration should have made Him too exhausted to carry that cross any distance at all. But they didn't.

Why? Because the purpose of Christ on earth required that He stay alive until all things were fulfilled in the scriptures. I know that there is a principle and promise of supernatural physical strength at work for those who are obediently carrying out the Father's will in their heart but need physical help to do it. I know God has done this for me.

In chapter one I visited the scene in the hospital where my "delicate petal" was born. In hindsight, as I revisit my first week at home with her, I can testify to the truth of God's promise of providing ever-present help and meeting every need, even when we are unaware that He is doing it.

I remember being extremely hungry and sleep-deprived, as the baby was not yet sleeping through the night. One day late in the morning I was at the kitchen sink bathing and washing my tiny infant's hair. I was ignoring the doctor's instructions to stay off my feet so I could heal and recover. My sense of self-worth was so low at that time that I didn't believe that I could take time for myself to rest, recover, and heal.

Anyway, as I was giving her a bath and beginning to wash her hair, the phone rang and woke up my other two toddlers. I didn't answer the phone because I had just gotten a little "gentle" baby wash in her eye and needed to tend to that while calming the other two who were startled by the phone.

The phone kept ringing! Usually around the forth or fifth ring people assume no one is there and hang up…but it kept ringing! Suddenly, I got a stabbing pain in my back, as though I were going into labor all over again. As I winced in pain, I heard the sound of a closing car door in the driveway at the church next door.

Due to the constant fray of our house and me, this sound typically triggered a great degree of anxiety. I did dread visitors I wasn't prepared to receive. So there was the anxiety gripping my heart as the loud phone continued ringing and the two toddlers clinging and that cheap "gentle" baby wash unyielding to my efforts at rinsing my baby's hair that nearly made me accept the dare to jump over the EDGE! I wasn't dressed to say the least and definitely not looking very preachers'-wife-like.

There was only a little shear curtain at the kitchen window and people could see in, if they made an effort and put their face close enough to the window. Quite a few did. Although it typically made me giggle to see the fog created by nosey, hot breath of the "curious," I was definitely not laughing now.

I started to stress out and panic in a way I never had before. At the sound of the gate opening, the two toddlers ran into one of the back rooms, and I grabbed the soapy bubbly baby and whisked her upstairs but not before soaking the floor with my blood!

As I called down to the children to go watch TV in the living room (far away from the sight on the kitchen floor) I was crying so hard from the stress of those moments that it certainly prolonged the healing of my frail body.

I was a physical wreck. Though there were times when I would be led to believe I could get some rest or walk outside for a few minutes to "get a break," I really couldn't. It never seemed to work out. I would hear the children wail within minutes, if not seconds, of my departure and immediately stop whatever I was doing and jump back to check things out. Something about the sound they made when they cried made me urgent in my response to them.

Upon going back into the house, he would angrily exit, grumbling: "Janeen, why do you always second-guess what I am doing or feel the need to intervene. Fine then, you take care of it all!"

Too often they were crying because he had not temperature checked the bottle before giving it to them. Too hot! They would be placed on their backs to nurse the bottle without help.

I wasted my time in trying to prepare for my "break." I would feed them and change their diapers before I left and request my "break" to coincide with their rigid nap schedule. But inevitably, if the baby was asleep and he wanted to play, he would dismiss my plea for help and "doctoral dissertation" on the need to "maintain their schedule." I would be in agony dealing with his decision to wake them and throw them off schedule AGAIN!

If I took a nap for a "break," the "ready" beep of the microwave made me jump and run. About two years after the bottle phase ended in our home the "ready" beep of the microwave still disturbed me.

It wasn't only that he would give them "hot bottles"…he was a gun owner, too. He had many guns. Let me just say that at this time he did not own a gun cabinet for his arsenal and stored them in creative locations that, to my horror, were easily accessible to the children. There were also food debris and dishes, including steak knives and silverware, on the floors around the area he reclined during his "watch."

They could have been crying for a lot of reasons. I jumped and stopped whatever "break" activity I was doing every time I heard them cry. And more often than not, every time I jumped to attend to them, they and I were thankful that I did. All this to say, the "break" I would take was really no break at all because rest and relaxation had nothing to do with it.

I was a physical wreck! Trembling was a natural phenomenon for me during this time. I became aware that God was empowering me with Calvary Strength when I awakened with the left side of my facial muscles sagging just a smidgen lower than the facial muscles on my right side. My body was telling me (in more ways than one) that it had had enough! God was with me all along.

Some women might have handled my dilemma with ease, but that season in my life nearly killed me. The point is still the same: God will endow those who are operating according to His will with whatever they need to achieve His purpose for their life, including supernatural physical strength.

What I know is that there were three babies counting on me for their very survival. God provided for His purpose for them by granting me gracious Calvary Strength, providing and privileging me with physical ability beyond what I could do. In addition to my three babies' survival, God had more in the earth for me to do. He sustains me.

CHAPTER 8

Now What?

"So Jonah went out of the city, and sat on the east side of
the city, and there made him a booth, and sat under it
in the shadow, till he might see what would become of
the city."

(Jonah 4:5 KJV)

Now WHAT? We are at the end—the end of Jonah's journey as
well as the end of this testimony of my journey to discover this dimension of God's Love for me. It all began with three central
movements to this discovery. First, I acknowledged my disobedience; second, I discovered prayer; and third, I practiced the discipline of obedience. At last I was to glean the following lessons
from the verse in Jonah above: Be merciful, live forgiven, and
reach back.

Be Merciful
What was Jonah looking for? Based on God's response to Jonah
in the last verse of Jonah chapter 4, I think Jonah was holding out
in hopes of seeing the outpouring of God's wrath on his enemies,
the Ninevites. When selfish anger at God's mercy toward another is present in a servant of God, I call it a bad case of the Jonah Syndrome.

It would appear from Jonah's sullen behavior that he lost
sight of the incredible mercy God had just extended to him
through safe passage and deliverance by a miraculous fish subma-

rine and being given a second chance to obey what God commanded him to do. I was inclined to think that the breeze and scent blowing off the nearby Tigris River would serve as a reminder of the journey that God just brought him through and cause him to embrace and demonstrate at least a modest measure of mercy being bestowed to the Ninevites through his act of service to them. They were headed for total damnation and destruction because they didn't know any better than their heathen ways! Are there some folks that should not receive mercy from the Lord? Do I forget God's mercy toward me too quickly and selfishly resent when He doles out gobs of it to people whom I think don't deserve it?

> *"The Lord is not slack concerning his promise, as some men count slackness; but is longsuffering to us-ward, not willing that any should perish, but that all should come to repentance."*
>
> *(2 Peter 3:9 KJV)*

God used the gourd plant as a catalyst to the manifestation of the Jonah Syndrome as it exposed the human heart's selfish inclination to resent His mercy when it is showered upon those perceived as "undeserving." Jonah did not procure the seed, till the ground, or plant and nurture the tree to maturity, yet he benefited from God's merciful provision of some much-needed shade against the sweltering heat from the sun. Though God provided for Jonah's great need, Jonah didn't even bother to thank God. He was so consumed with the possibility that the service God commanded him to perform to his enemies may result in God's extending them mercy that he resented the very nature of who God is (4:2-3). God's judgments are always a reflection of man's heart, but God's goodness isn't!

Live Forgiven

I would have felt so guilty after God asked me those questions at the end of the book. It may have been difficult to get up and get going again. I have to repent and live forgiven. Unlike God, we are given to our memories and the enemy exploits this area of human weakness. Guilt can be disabling. Don't let the enemy win!

"So, be disciplined to renew the mind with the cleansing
of the Word."

(Philippians 4:8-9)

Forgive me for craving the traditional American "happy ending" to this very dramatic book of the Bible. I found the ending of the book anti-climactic!

Only silence from Jonah?

Not even a dash for it?

A big altar call with Jonah repenting and bolting out in tears with his hair flying in the breeze to enlist in frontline duty in the Lord's Army would have satisfied my flair for the dramatic, but no such thing happened!

That's how it all ends: Silence!

So I ask you, my friend, how will you answer the Lord? *Your* Lord!

Will you embrace His righteousness and trust His sovereign rule?

Will you resent His extension of mercy toward someone who hurt you?

To answer these questions favoarably to the Lord's will is easier said than done. But don't be bound by guilt and shame because you are sick with a bad case of the Jonah Syndrome. As well, don't allow the ailment you are struggling with to be an excuse to stay sick. As it did with Jonah, this syndrome will cause you to lose sight of the very nature of God as your focus and energy are preoccupied with resentment. Make God the center of your attention, and it will cure the most severe (even terminal) case of the Jonah Syndrome. God loves His children when they are sick or afflicted just the same as if they were "perfect." Don't be bound with your illness. If you have a case of the Jonah Syndrome, live free by understanding that God is a forgiving God and is more than able to love you to health.

> *"I had fainted, unless I had believed to see the goodness of the LORD in the land of the living. Wait on the LORD: be of good courage, and he shall strengthen thine heart: wait, I say, on the LORD."*
>
> *(Psalm 27:13-14 KJV)*

I don't see God the same as I did before—and, no, it is not because I got any of that icky ejection residue in my eyes!

If any groom has the right to divorce His bride, it is Christ. He has had to put up with the church (you and me)! He is the consummate model of unconditional love. You may be saying, "He's God, though." And I definitely know that, but let me tell you this: Because He is God and He is all-knowing, He knows what we can handle, and in His wisdom He would not ask us to serve in a way we could not—apart from Him. But we can only do it with His help, with His perspective, and with His Love.

He who knew no sin became sin for us all so that we could inherit His grace. So that we can sin no more? No, but so that we wouldn't have to!

We have committed adultery time and time again! We have lied, talked Him down, stolen money from Him, held more than one love in our heart, gave what He provided to our other lover, killed His children, and yet He loves us still! As if we did none of those things at all.

He still looks at us longingly with great affection and passion and Love. The twinkle is still in His eyes for us. He holds nothing back from us. He speaks and protects us and courts us still. He brags on us and shows us off because He is proud of us! Still and all, still and all! So I encourage you to get on with the business of living your life as one of His forgiven children.

In return, what shall I give to the Love of my life? The Lover of my soul? How can I demonstrate my gratitude, my repentant heart, and love to the One who is Love?

"If ye love me, keep my commandments."

(John 14:15 KJV)

His children should obey His commandments not as a legalist would, for His holiness would always keep the scales unbalanced. We will never ever be able to pay Him back for all the Love and grace He has given, we can only love Him back as He has asked us to through our devoted service to Him and honoring His purpose for our life. Not just for the tangible benefits our obedience brings, but for the benefit of indwelling constantly in His almighty presence and the renewing power it provides our spirit.

After all that we have been through, what is there to fret over? He forgives me and loves me. I will not carry a burden of guilt because I don't have to repeat what has already been done for me through the work of Christ on the cross. I am whole and clean and acceptable to Christ. What is left? Nothing. It is finished.

If I am good enough for *Him*, who cares what any man may think?

"What shall we then say to these things? If God be for us,
who can be against us? He that spared not his own
Son, but delivered him up for us all, how shall he not

*with him also freely give us all things? Who shall lay
any thing to the charge of God's elect? It is God that
justifieth. Who is he that condemneth? It is Christ that
died, yea rather, that is risen again, who is even at the
right hand of God, who also maketh intercession for us.
Who shall separate us from the love of Christ? shall
tribulation, or distress, or persecution, or famine, or
nakedness, or peril, or sword? As it is written, For thy
sake we are killed all the day long; we are accounted as
sheep for the slaughter. Nay, in all these things we are
more than conquerors through him that loved us. For I
am persuaded, that neither death, nor life, nor angels,
nor principalities, nor powers, nor things present, nor
things to come, Nor height, nor depth, nor any other
creature, shall be able to separate us from the love of
God, which is in Christ Jesus our Lord."*

(Romans 8:31-39 KJV)

Reach Back

Each of us has our own custom-made struggles and circumstances, but all of us have them just the same. Some would rather
examine these struggles and circumstances for the sole purpose
of rating themselves according to how "hard" they have it and
how "well" they have managed to endure it, but to be admired is
the brilliance of God. That's right, He is so brilliant that He has
tailored each journey for everyone, to accomplish His ultimate
goal: to glorify Himself.

Perhaps you think that seems to be pretty cruel and selfish because it is this tailored fit that presses in and can hurt so bad. But
did you know that the greatest glory to Him is a victorious *you?*

Let's look again at Jonah. God spared no needed detail to
make Jonah an effective evangelist to the Ninevites. Imagine be-

ing a Ninevite and worshipping the "fish god" (as the Ninevites did) and seeing a prophet of the true God being coughed up onto dry land by the biggest fish you may have ever seen. What an awesome sight that must have been! It would have made a believer out of me. In spite of himself and for the glory of God, Jonah was raised up "out of a symbol" of a dead thing in faith and works to herald God's awesome message of grace and repentance to those who needed to hear it. God looked beyond the faults and saw the needs.

So go ahead and reach back. Put an exclamation point on the freedom you have found in your own giant fish voyage and deepening walk with Christ by telling a friend. Your testimony is so powerful, no matter how bizarre it may appear on the outside because someone (if not many people) are waiting for you to tell it and need to hear it.

Telling a friend will also provide a reminder and encouragement to you as you recall how God indeed brought you out of the belly of your great fish, whatever detailed form that may have been

Additionally, during those moments when the enemy tempts you to overlook the hand of mercy God extended to you or the thought that perhaps your relationship with Christ isn't really liberating and causes your commitment to wane, your declarations of the mighty works God performed in your life to draw you closer to Himself is sure to blow powerful wind into your sails to move you forward! Testify of your firsthand knowledge of His initiation and passionate desire to provide you with the security and freedom that only a walk with Him can bring. Share the stories of God's care in your life even when it didn't *feel* as though that was what He was doing. Go ahead and celebrate the promises of God in your life with the fruit of your lips boldy I will testify to you that I know that I am God's beloved daughter:

- God is Love
- He loves you
- He loves me

"And they overcame him by the blood of the Lamb, and by the word of their testimony; and they loved not their lives unto the death."

(Revelations 12:11 KJV)

The Book of Jonah

King James Version

Jonah 1

1Now the word of the LORD came unto Jonah the son of Amittai, saying,

2Arise, go to Nineveh, that great city, and cry against it; for their wickedness is come up before me.

3But Jonah rose up to flee unto Tarshish from the presence of the LORD, and went down to Joppa; and he found a ship going to Tarshish: so he paid the fare thereof, and went down into it, to go with them unto Tarshish from the presence of the LORD.

4But the LORD sent out a great wind into the sea, and there was a mighty tempest in the sea, so that the ship was like to be broken.

5Then the mariners were afraid, and cried every man unto his god, and cast forth the wares that were in the ship into the sea, to lighten it of them. But Jonah was gone down into the sides of the ship; and he lay, and was fast asleep.

6So the shipmaster came to him, and said unto him, What meanest thou, O sleeper? arise, call upon thy God, if so be that God will think upon us, that we perish not.

7And they said every one to his fellow, Come, and let us cast lots, that we may know for whose cause this evil is upon us. So they cast lots, and the lot fell upon Jonah.

8Then said they unto him, Tell us, we pray thee, for whose cause this evil is upon us; What is thine occupation? and whence comest thou? what is thy country? and of what people art thou?

9And he said unto them, I am an Hebrew; and I fear the LORD, the God of heaven, which hath made the sea and the dry land.

10Then were the men exceedingly afraid, and said unto him. Why hast thou done this? For the men knew that he fled from the presence of the LORD, because he had told them.

11Then said they unto him, What shall we do unto thee, that the sea may be calm unto us? for the sea wrought, and was tempestuous.

12And he said unto them, Take me up, and cast me forth into the sea; so shall the sea be calm unto you: for I know that for my sake this great tempest is upon you.

13Nevertheless the men rowed hard to bring it to the land; but they could not: for the sea wrought, and was tempestuous against them.

14Wherefore they cried unto the LORD, and said, We beseech thee, O LORD, we beseech thee, let us not perish for this man's life, and lay not upon us innocent blood: for thou, O LORD, hast done as it pleased thee.

15So they took up Jonah, and cast him forth into the sea: and the sea ceased from her raging.

16Then the men feared the LORD exceedingly, and offered a sacrifice unto the LORD, and made vows.

17Now the LORD had prepared a great fish to swallow up Jonah. And Jonah was in the belly of the fish three days and three nights.

Jonah 2

1Then Jonah prayed unto the LORD his God out of the fish's belly,

2And said, I cried by reason of mine affliction unto the LORD, and he heard me; out of the belly of hell cried I, and thou heardest my voice.

3For thou hadst cast me into the deep, in the midst of the seas; and the floods compassed me about: all thy billows and thy waves passed over me.

4Then I said, I am cast out of thy sight; yet I will look again toward thy holy temple.

5The waters compassed me about, even to the soul: the depth closed me round about, the weeds were wrapped about my head.

6I went down to the bottoms of the mountains; the earth with her bars was about me for ever: yet hast thou brought up my life from corruption, O LORD my God.

7When my soul fainted within me I remembered the LORD: and my prayer came in unto thee, into thine holy temple.

8They that observe lying vanities forsake their own mercy.

9But I will sacrifice unto thee with the voice of thanksgiving; I will pay that that I have vowed. Salvation is of the LORD.

10And the LORD spake unto the fish, and it vomited out Jonah upon the dry land.

Jonah 3

1And the word of the LORD came unto Jonah the second time, saying,

2Arise, go unto Nineveh, that great city, and preach unto it the preaching that I bid thee.

3So Jonah arose, and went unto Nineveh, according to the word of the LORD. Now Nineveh was an exceeding great city of three days' journey.

4And Jonah began to enter into the city a day's journey, and he cried, and said, Yet forty days, and Nineveh shall be overthrown.

5So the people of Nineveh believed God, and proclaimed a fast, and put on sackcloth, from the greatest of them even to the least of them.

6For word came unto the king of Nineveh, and he arose from his throne, and he laid his robe from him, and covered him with sackcloth, and sat in ashes.

7And he caused it to be proclaimed and published through Nineveh by the decree of the king and his nobles, saying, Let neither man nor beast, herd nor flock, taste any thing: let them not feed, nor drink water:

8But let man and beast be covered with sackcloth, and cry mightily unto God: yea, let them turn every one from his evil way, and from the violence that is in their hands.

9Who can tell if God will turn and repent, and turn away from his fierce anger, that we perish not?

10And God saw their works, that they turned from their evil way; and God repented of the evil, that he had said that he would do unto them; and he did it not.

Jonah 4

1But it displeased Jonah exceedingly, and he was very angry.

2And he prayed unto the LORD, and said, I pray thee, O LORD, was not this my saying, when I was yet in my country? Therefore I fled before unto Tarshish: for I knew that thou art a gracious God, and merciful, slow to anger, and of great kindness, and repentest thee of the evil.

3Therefore now, O LORD, take, I beseech thee, my life from me; for it is better for me to die than to live.

4Then said the LORD, Doest thou well to be angry?

5So Jonah went out of the city, and sat on the east side of the city, and there made him a booth, and sat under it in the shadow, till he might see what would become of the city.

6And the LORD God prepared a gourd, and made it to come up over Jonah, that it might be a shadow over his head, to deliver him from his grief. So Jonah was exceeding glad of the gourd.

7But God prepared a worm when the morning rose the next day, and it smote the gourd that it withered.

8And it came to pass, when the sun did arise, that God prepared a vehement east wind; and the sun beat upon the head of Jonah, that he fainted, and wished in himself to die, and said, It is better for me to die than to live.

9And God said to Jonah, Doest thou well to be angry for the gourd? And he said, I do well to be angry, even unto death.

10Then said the LORD, Thou hast had pity on the gourd, for the which thou hast not laboured, neither madest it grow; which came up in a night, and perished in a night:

11And should not I spare Nineveh, that great city, wherein are more than sixscore thousand persons that cannot discern between their right hand and their left hand; and also much cattle?

References & Reading

Blackaby, H.T., & King, C.V.K. (2004). *Experiencing God:Knowing and doing the will of God.* Nashville: Broadman & Holman.

Cloud, Dr. H., & Townsend, J. (1992). *Boundaries.* Grand Rapids: Zondervan Publishing House.

Deen, E. (1955). *All of the Women of the Bible.* New York: Harper & Row.

Evans, A.T. (2005). *Let it Go: Breaking free from fear and anxiety.* Chicago: Moody.

Franklin, J. (2008). *Fasting: Opening the door to a deeper, more intimate, more powerful relationship with God.* Lake Mary, FL: Charisma House.

Kuykendall, C. (1955, 2000). *Loving and Letting Go: The Key to Being a Good Mom.* Grand Rapids: Zondervan.

Lutzer, E. (2000). *Getting closer to God: Keys to spiritual intimacy from the life of Moses.* Ann Arbor: Servant Publications.

Morris, Henry Madison (1985). *Biblical Basis for Modern Science.* Grand Rapids: Baker Publishing Group

Ortlund, A. (1977, 1984). *Disciplines of a Beautiful Woman.* Waco, TX: Word.

Smalley, G. & Trent, J. (1990, 1992). *The Two Sides of Love: Twenty specific ways to build unbreakable bonds with your family and friends.* Irving, TX: Word.

Wilson, P.B. (1990). *Liberated Through Submission: The Ultimate Paradox.* Eugene, OR: Harvest House.

ABOUT THE AUTHOR

Janeen Michael-Lanier, a native of Pasadena, California, now resides with her husband and three children in Atlanta, Georgia. She currently serves as the worship leader and worship arts director in her local church.

Printed in the United States
215683BV00001B/4/P